GOD, YOU and LOVE

My Journey of Spiritual Discovery

GOD, YOU and LOVE

My Journey of Spiritual Discovery

Recorded by

HANS WUELFERT

Regency Press (London and New York) Ltd
Chaucer House, Chaucer Business Park,
Kemsing, Sevenoaks, Kent TN15 6PW

First published 2001

ISBN 07212 0972 6

Printed in England by Buckland Press Ltd,
Barwick Road, Dover CT17 0LG

PREFACE

In the last thirty years, I must have read hundreds of manuscripts on Spiritualism, the paranormal and spirituality in general. To be honest (and this is not to denigrate their authors), many are somewhat run-of-the-mill, often lacking that vital spark of originality which compels one to read them with a sense of urgency and excited expectation.

Hans Wuelfert was born in Germany, though now lives in Australia. Yet this book is not so much concerned with this world, but in a sense the next since he obviously appreciates that we are all spiritual beings temporarily in physical form.

Much of *God, You and Love* is based upon the Bible. Yet the author's interpretation of the happenings it chronicles is not only interesting, but also challenging, perhaps even controversial in part. This, surely, is what books should do by challenging commonly held views, offering a different, fresh and original approach, one that stimulates readers intellectually, spiritually and morally.

Another notable aspect of *God, You and Love* is the massive amount of research and thought that have been painstakingly put into this title. It has obviously taken Mr Wuelfert many years to distil his thoughts. The result is an equally thought-provoking book which allows one to see Biblical and other events in a new perspective.

'The Spirit is the breath of life for all of us, no matter how we prefer to be aware of the Spirit, no matter where we prefer to be aware of the Spirit, even no matter whether we are aware of the Spirit at all,' writes Mr Wuelfert. 'The Spirit is totally unavoidable.'

Were this simple but profound message appreciated on a world-wide basis, how very different life on earth would be, for humanity would then truly realise it is a brotherhood of man, disparate nations linked by a common denominator.

Mr Wuelfert has sub-titled his book *My Journey of Spiritual Discovery*. May it spur and stimulate you on your journey, too.

Tony Ortzen,
Editor, *Two Worlds*.
London, 2001

DEDICATION

Since this writing was mine only for the recording,

may I dedicate it to my fellow-men

for whom it was ultimately destined

Hans Wuelfert

CONTENTS

Part Two

PART ONE

FOREWORD

Even though this book is not an account of my own thoughts, I feel I should give a certain amount of personal background.

I grew up in Germany. My parents, my sister and I were a closely-knit family for which faith and love provided a strong basis. After my paternal grandfather's death there was discord among one side of the family which made life very difficult for us. The situation became more complex and even threatening when my father initially would have nothing to do with the national-socialist party. In retrospect, I can say that these traumatic events made our faith and our love for each other stronger and more precious.

We did not have a close connection with the Lutheran Church, the only church in our protestant village. The main reasons were that my mother came from a religious group which was not organised like a church and that my father was a strong individualist, even as far as his belief was concerned. When under the Hitler regime attempts were made to establish a national Protestant Church with strong national-socialist overtones, my parents seized the opportunity 'to be Christians and good Germans at the same time'. However, this church was a complete failure.

In my mid-teens I saw active service in the Second World War and at its end I was taken prisoner. I spent some time in an Eastern European country, an experience which reduced me physically to a wreck and as a person to a level which was almost not human any more. My uppermost memory of that time, however, is the wonderful kindness shown to me by a local family. All the other memories have faded. I have ever since felt a strong affection for the people of that country.

What I have said so far may show why, in my experience, the caring relationship with our fellow-man, with an individual and with a group, is of paramount importance. Loving one's own family, one's friends and one's people need not and must not create the necessity to hate others. We know that we are all children of God. We know that we must not love the one and hate the other. That is the Will of God. Thus our relationship with our fellow-man is closely interwoven with our relationship with God. In reverse, our relationship with God profoundly influences our relationship with our fellow-man. And God's relationship with us here on earth? Surely, God Himself complies with His Own Will – He is His Will – and does not love the one and hate the other. He loves us all.

At this point I would like to give thanks to God who granted me a good and a rich life. I greatly appreciate my family and relatives, my chosen brother and my friends in the old country. My wife and family are wonderful; I am grateful to them for their love, kindness and understanding. To my relatives and friends in these parts I say a sincere thank you. In particular I would like to express my gratitude to a very special friend of our family who helped me find my path and gave me a flying start.

Shortly before my mother passed away more than twenty years ago, she gave me an annual publication of the Evangelical Churches, Lutheran and Reformed, of Germany and Switzerland. It is in the form of a calendar with systematic daily Bible readings which are accompanied by commentaries and other relevant writing.

Till about three years ago I read the Bible in a seemingly naïve way, or perhaps I was shielded by my faith. Because I had been taught by my parents and because my whole life has been proof that God is the God of Love, the statements in the Bible about man's abject and sinful nature, his constant danger of falling victim to Satan, his fear of not being good enough to be acceptable to God, his prospects of the Last Judgement and possibly of eternal damnation and suffering in hell – all this just did not register with me. And I am so grateful it did not.

As the result of a powerful spiritual experience during a Reiki seminar about three years ago, I became absolutely convinced that reincarnation takes place. A year later, during meditations, I was shown scenes of some of my past lives, two in South America, and one in Israel among people who were with Jesus. Around the same time spirits of four relatives, as servants of the Lord, came into my life as my guardians and helpers. I feel now that the wonderful spiritual experience of a visit to

12

South America, especially Peru, a few months later rounded off the preparation for me to record this writing.

So far, the manuscript has taken about two years to write. While I wrote I was being taught. Prior to that I could not have imagined that anything like this could happen to me and I am still astounded and will always be humbly grateful. Prior to that I would not and I could not have thought the way I think now. Prior to that I had no idea that I could ever accept and believe what I have been given to write. The change within me has been gradual; it has been a process of growing; it has been progress along the path of my spiritual journey; it has been part of the constant change which takes place because the Will of God is at work. May the reader find also that there is constant change and development because the Will of God is at work.

Acknowledgments

The production of this book was assured by a great deal of help which was readily given. I have very much appreciated Rosmarie's consistent support and encouragement. When the manuscript was ready to be put on computer, Gloria offered to do this painstaking work for which I thank her sincerely. I would also like to record my gratitude to Patricia for her expert advice and for suggesting such an appropriate title for the book. Last, but not least, I am deeply grateful to my wife Helen for her practical help throughout the time of writing and for coping so well with a writer husband.

Note to the reader

The use of small letters and capital letters in this writing with reference to God, Jesus, the Holy Ghost and The One is not arbitrary.

Consider the expression: 'God is a just God.' This means that God's actions are like those of a human being. In this case they are just, God shows justice.

Contrast this with the statement: 'We are assured of God's Unconditional Love.' This implies that God is not a human being and He does not show love like a human being. In fact, God Himself is His Unconditional Love.

This particular aspect will become much clearer to the reader as he makes his way through the book.

Australia,
August 1995

PSALM 23

The Lord is my shepherd, I shall not want;
he makes me lie down in green pastures.
He leads me beside still waters,
he restores my soul.
He leads me in the paths of righteousness
for his name's sake.
Even though I walk through
the valley of the shadow of death, I fear no evil;
for thou art with me;
thy rod and thy staff,
they comfort me.
Thou preparest a table before me
in the presence of my enemies;
thou anointest my head with oil, my cup overflows.
Surely goodness and mercy shall follow me
all the days of my life;
and I shall dwell in the house of the LORD for ever.

The purpose of this writing

There is no purpose in this writing other than to state what had to be said.

It was written for its own sake.

It does not present itself as a tool to be used because a tool can be used in so many ways for so many different purposes, some of which may serve the interests of the user only. It is not a ways and means for someone's plans and ambitions.

This writing does not present the writer's personal thoughts. He merely wrote down what was given to him.

This writing as such does not consider itself to be antagonistic to ideas from which it differs. It is not hostile either to institutions which are based on these ideas. It does not criticise. It does not judge. It is not concerned with other ideas and other concepts. It does not tell anybody what to do and what not to do. It is simply there.

A person's acceptance or non-acceptance of what is stated in this writing is entirely his choice. If somebody decides to ignore it, that again is entirely his choice. To make a choice is to exercise one's freedom.

The divine nature of the soul

The soul is encased in the human body. We believe that it was put into the body and when the body dies the soul will be released.

Quite clearly, the soul is not part of the body. Quite clearly, the soul is not restricted to a measurable time span. Quite clearly, it existed before it appeared in the body and, quite clearly, it continues to exist after it has left the body. Within the capacity of our understanding we conclude that the soul is not of this world, that it is everlasting, that it is indestructible and, therefore, that it must be divine.

The word 'divine' to us can have various meanings, such as 'relating

17

to God, devoted to God, coming from God, being like God, being God'. Of these definitions only two are relevant to our considerations. As we are thinking and talking about what the soul 'is', the two expressions containing the word 'being' are the ones we have to consider. Let us begin with 'being like God'. This refers to the situation where there is God and beside this God, literally by His side, there are other beings who have the same characteristics and qualities which God has. However, the Bible tells us that there is only one God. Therefore when we consider our soul the only proper description would be 'being God'. Since there is only one God we have to elaborate a little in order to accommodate this concept in our human thinking process. We have to say that our soul is part of the one God who put part of Himself into our body, who made it stay in our body and who will take it out of our body when this body dies.

Conflict between the soul and the body leads to sin

During our lifetime, because we are strongly influenced by the physical nature of our existence, such as need for food, clothing and shelter, our way of life can come into conflict with our soul. Since the physical nature of our existence normally goes beyond our basic requirements of food, clothing and shelter – with aspirations to wealth, fame and power, for instance – if these interests are pursued in violation of God's Commandments, the conflict with our soul definitely becomes a transgression, a sin.

Judgement for the believer and the non-believer according to the Bible

The Christian faith makes a point that with the hereafter there is unavoidable judgement. Christ tells us that we will be saved only by faith and the Grace of God; indeed, the believer will not have to go through judgement at all.(1)

This leaves us then with the concept of eternal damnation, of hell, for the souls of the non-believers who have to go through judgement, are found guilty and are condemned to eternal suffering as punishment for the sins committed on earth.

> (1)   Truly, truly, I say to you, he who hears my word and believes him who sent me, has eternal life; he does not come into judgement, but has passed from death to life. (John 5:24)

18

The soul does not go into judgement

Sins are committed in conflict with the soul, against the better judgement of the soul. The soul knows what is right and what is wrong, but the mind and the body either do not take notice or deliberately ignore the voice of the soul. Death on earth not only destroys the body, but also the human element of our personality. It is the human element of our personality which does not listen to the soul, to the God within the body. This results in an extraordinary situation. Only the soul can be condemned, not the body because the body is destroyed by death. That means the soul is found guilty of sins it could not prevent. Or could it have been that the body and mind managed to corrupt the soul and to implicate it in its sins? If the soul is not part of this world, if the soul is the God in us, it cannot even be touched by our human failings. Furthermore, if the soul were condemned through judgement by God, it would amount to God condemning part of Himself.

As the Son of God, Christ was and is part of God, part of the Trinity of God the Father, God the Son and God the Holy Ghost. Christ suffered on the cross, but not as punishment. He was not condemned for the sins He did not commit. It was an act of self-sacrifice, of incomprehensible self-sacrifice as a guarantee that man will be saved through his faith and the Grace of God.(1)

> (1)   Truly, truly I say to you, he who believes has eternal life. (John 6:47)
> Be merciful, even as your Father is merciful. (Luke 6:36)

Salvation of the living

If there is no judgement for the soul, if the God in us is above sin, how are we to understand the salvation of man through the sacrifice of our Lord Jesus on the cross? This salvation is promised us through the Bible as we know it. We hear this promise while we are still among the living. Because His promise does not relate to the hereafter, it must refer exclusively to our present worldly existence. It can apply only to the living man, Adam, the human being of soul, mind and body. This composite human being is assured deliverance from sin through his faith in God and through the Grace of God. Again the visible act of God who manifests His Grace to man who has to see and hear in order to believe,

19

to believe that – like the traditional unblemished lamb – Christ was literally sacrificed to cleanse us from our sins.

God our Father takes the initiative again. He offers us forgiveness. He does not ask us to perform to a certain standard of human achievement or worldly morality. The Lord loves a sinner who repents, a sinner who believes, a sinner who puts out his hand to receive the wonderful gift of forgiveness. This forgiveness marks the end of an episode and provides a new beginning. It takes the burden of regret, of shame, of guilt, of self-reproach from the conscience of man. Man's soul has been grieving with him just as much as the Heavenly Father has been grieving with him. Both rejoice like the good shepherd that the lost sheep has been found and returned to the safety of the flock under His watchful eyes.

How people come to faith

We must have a brief look at how people become believers. Some have experienced the opening up of their soul to the Word of God as an act of grace and favour by the Lord. They do not consider that it was through their own efforts or their own decision. This idea would also apply to people who are not aware of any such specific event, including those who have believed since early childhood. There are others who can name the date and the hour. Again there are the ones who made a conscious and deliberate decision that God would be the centre of their lives. In each case the acquisition of faith requires the existence of a soul.

Is it possible that the inability of somebody to believe is caused by the fact that this person has no soul? Is it possible that God created man 'not in His image'? Is it possible that He sent him into life as an 'animal' in human form? Surely, the answer must be 'no'.

Reincarnation

Reincarnation of a soul which, in a different body, is sent back into this world as punishment for sins committed in a previous life or several previous lives, would certainly restrict the process of justice to our life on earth. It would also empty of all its meaning the suffering and sacrifice of Christ on the cross. Furthermore, it would place a person's responsibility entirely on his shoulders which would condemn him for ever. Why for ever? In one life he would learn and make up for the mistakes and sins of a previous life, but his human nature would cause him to make new mistakes and commit more sins. Perfection cannot be achieved by a human being in this world.

The concept of reincarnation of a soul which is sent back into this world to continue the learning process does not attach the label of good or bad to the person's previous actions. The soul would come back in a different body simply to learn from its previous mistakes and to avoid them this time round. Is there a pre-determined length of the learning process? If there is not, there appear to be two possibilities. Firstly, the soul makes fewer and fewer mistakes in each subsequent life and when it has reached a 'satisfactory level of achievement' the cycle is terminated. The second possibility would be that, because of new mistakes being made, the learning process would never end and if it did end, it would do so through an outside intervention, through an intervention by God.

There is one fundamental flaw with these two ideas of reincarnation. Since the same soul is sent back into the world, it must have been the soul which made the mistakes in the previous life. The body is never sent back. If the soul is responsible for the mistakes is cannot be divine. If it is not divine it is of this world and therefore is subject to a beginning and an end. If the soul dies with the body there is no reincarnation and the soul would be located somewhere in the body. If the soul is the spiritual state of being produced by an organ of the body then it should be possible to name this organ.

This leaves us with the concept of reincarnation simply as the reappearance of a soul in another body without any condition or additional intent. This would agree with the divine nature of the soul: untarnished and eternal.

The growing awareness of the soul of its divine nature

The question of reincarnation has to be looked at from a different angle. What has been called a learning process here on earth needs clarification. This process is not an acquisition of skills necessary to cope with various situations involving either just the person himself or taking in also his interaction with his fellow-men and his environment. This process is in fact restricted to the soul becoming increasingly aware of itself, of its divine nature. When the soul is sent back to earth it is associated with certain human tasks deemed necessary to further this awareness. It may be concluded that these tasks had not been attempted in previous lifetimes or that they could not be carried out in a way which helped the soul along its path.

Even though the soul is part of God, it is not exactly like Him, it is not the Truth and it is not the Will, for instance. While the soul is in a human body it has to grow in its awareness of its divine nature till it is sufficiently conscious of itself to be permanently admitted to eternal life. This would be similar to the situation referred to in 1 John 3:2 '...but we know that when he appears we shall be like him, for we shall see him as he is'. The words 'like him' are to be understood as to mean 'sufficiently like Him to be able to endure His Presence'.

In eternal life, too, there are various stages of growth and awareness for the soul to go through. There the journey also leads from level to level, from plane to plane.

The question of a person with a dormant soul has arisen before. In this case the soul has not yet begun the process of becoming aware of itself, resulting in the absence of any active relationship with the Creator. This condition which may last a whole human lifetime makes absolutely no difference to the dignity and holiness of that person in his own right.

The soul as a governing spirit and as a receiving spirit

We have to think of the soul as part of our God, of our portion of His Holiness. Nevertheless, the soul is in us not only as a governing spirit, but also as a receiving spirit. It attempts to counsel the mind/body part of each person. However, it also receives, records and accepts the essence of this person's activities: thoughts, feelings and actions. We may best call it a human soul: the God in us exercising His divine influence, but at the same time being exposed to the person's activities.

There is a spiritual aspect to each facet of our human activities. An activity is not only a flow of energy in a particular form and in a given intensity from the person towards a receiving fellow-man or a part of the environment. An activity is also the manifestation, the embodiment, of a spiritual value. This spiritual value returns to the person the activity came from. This spiritual essence of the person's activities was created by the person himself in the first place. Now it is absorbed and makes its influence felt on the inner being. This gives the person control over his spiritual development and reminds us of the words 'as you sow, so shall you reap'. Perhaps we can compare this process with the growing pattern of a tree trunk. The new growth appears as rings around the already existing core. The God-given part of this soul, the core, does not change.

22

What man can add is simply something on the outside. The comparison cannot be continued logically to the very end. Instead, we must come back to the term already used, a human soul, which in itself is not acceptable in terms of logic. Logic would classify it as an absurd notion. We would do well to remember here that the figure of Christ defied the logic of the Pharisees who could not accommodate it in their thinking and belief patterns that He was the Son of God yet stood in front of them as the son of a human being, of Mary. This, to them, was utterly absurd.

Whatever a person adds to the outside of his soul can be considered to be of a varying degree of density. These additions would range from the high density and depressing weight of values returned from activities which are evil in the eyes of the Lord to the low density and uplifting buoyancy of values returned from actions which are pleasing in the eyes of the Lord.

The significance of Christ's death

At this point we have to consider two questions. The first one is: 'Did Christ have to die to save our souls?' The answer must be 'no' because thanks to its divine nature our soul will never be endangered. The situation just will not arise that it will have to be saved. Our soul is on an entirely different plane because God is on an entirely different plane.

The second question asks: 'Did Christ have to die – that is did God have to become a human being – to be put to death and to be resurrected to show us convincingly that there is eternal life after death?' The answer is 'yes'. Every now and again the people around Christ asked for a sign, something they could see, hear, or touch, as a basis for their belief. Christ Himself quite often used parables to present His teaching in a way which made it easier for the people to understand and believe. These parables pictured situations of real life experience of Christ's contemporaries. Still in our days they are vivid and compelling situations which perfectly convey the intended meaning. This is why Christ's death and resurrection had to be acted out in front of these people to prove that there is eternal life after death.(1)

At the same time Christ's death was the tangible and convincing proof of the unimaginable and Unconditional Love of our Heavenly Father for all of us. There is eternal life for all of us not because of our own doing and effort, but by the Grace of our Lord who sent His Son into the world. The Son did His Father's Will, died on the cross, in front of witnesses and after His resurrection appeared to many. It was tangible experience.

The same principle applies to His teaching. It had to be spread by word of mouth and as written communication in the thought and language patterns of the people of those days. His message and purpose of His coming into this world had to be brought down to our human level to make us understand. Indeed, this is one of the reasons why Christ came into this world, this is one of the reasons why God chose His Son to be God and man at the same time. As the Son of God and as the son of man Christ is the bridge between us and our Heavenly Father.

> (1)   Now Thomas, one of the twelve, called the Twin, was not with them when Jesus came. So the other disciples told him, 'We have seen the Lord.' But he said to them, 'Unless I see in his hands the print of the nails, and place my finger in the mark of the nails, and place my hand in his side, I will not believe.' (John 20:24,25).

Punishment and reward take place in this world

What of the idea of punishment and reward? We must state right from the beginning that these two words are our own terms, our own concepts which we choose because they are suitable for us. In the true sense they involve an outside agent who would act according to his will or judgement. We must discard this and accept the following: the inner happiness which we could think of as reward and the inner unhappiness which we could think of as punishment are the results of our own actions, of our own decisions which we make on the basis of our inner freedom.

With the believer, that is with the person who listens to his soul, the positive results of his actions are of the kind which he enjoys in his life here on earth. In God or Jesus he always has a friend to turn to in prayer, to thank and to ask, in happiness and in sorrow. When in doubt, we obtain guidance and reassurance, in despair we are given hope. We journey through life guided, protected, helped, uplifted, comforted and in the fellowship of our brothers and sisters in Christ. Death, the end of the journey, appears in an entirely different light: it is not the end, it is but a new beginning. Because of the Grace of God in these and other blessings, a believer's life is so much richer, happier and filled with meaning. Indeed the Kingdom of God is in the midst of us.(1)

If the Kingdom of God is in our midst, if the positive results of one's decisions are within, then there is the possibility of the negative results of one's decisions being within also. This would be according to the words 'as you sow, so shall you reap'. It is sometimes not obvious, it is sometimes even impossible to imagine that somebody who does not treat his neighbour as he would wish to be treated himself would have a guilty conscience, would be unhappy within himself because of what he has done and may even do again. A criminal would live in fear of being found out, the greedy would not be able to enjoy what they have because their greed would always spur them on to acquire more. These persons would be obsessed and possessed, they would not be free, they would be slaves to themselves, they would indeed be suffering.

(1) Being asked by the Pharisees when the kingdom of God was coming, he answered them. 'The kingdom of God is not coming with signs to be observed; nor will they say, 'Lo, here it is!' or 'There!' for behold the kingdom of God is in the midst of you' (or 'within you'). (Luke 17:20,21)
Martin Luther translated: '. . . *sehet, das Reich Gottes ist inwendig in euch*', which means: '. . . behold, the kingdom of God is right within you.'.

Spirit, mind and body and their interaction

'The spirit is willing but the flesh is weak' is to mean that the spirit which we may also call the soul has a will to do what is right in the eyes of the Lord. Its efforts can be thwarted by the flesh which we may also call the body. It is interesting that there is no separate mention of the mind. This omission, if we may call it such, can be explained with the fact that the mind is a function of the brain and can therefore be grouped with the body. A very clear line is drawn here between the spirit and the mind, relegating the mind to the physical. The mind seems to be the link between the soul and the body. It is actually more than that, it is also the 'master-mind' of the body. There is close co-operation between the mind and the body, each influencing the other and their joint agreement deciding the direction in which they are going to move.

The mind can be in touch with the soul as deeply as it wishes, constantly or off and on, regardless of the topics which come up in the mind. The mind can be selective to suit its own inclinations. Its attitude can be influenced by its communication with the body, or be shaped by the messages it receives from the soul. The mind can be persuaded by the soul to rise to higher levels and make this aspiration its second nature, transmitting this elevating influence into the body. On the other hand, the mind can turn most of its attention to the wishes and requirements of the body and guide it along the path of mutual benefit. The mind's commitment to either the soul or the body can vary even to such an extent that there is a complete and radical change of direction in the behaviour of the person.

If the mind/body takes note of its constant monitor, the soul, then soul and mind/body can live in harmony. The latter will not be based on a categorical agreement between the two units which will serve for a whole lifetime. There will be adjustments, constant minor or major changes, a continued play of varying forces pointing in varying directions. Nevertheless, the two units will be at ease with each other.

On the other hand, the mind/body has to accommodate the tensions which arise between itself and the soul. There may be repercussions of a sometimes completely unexpected nature in the least likely parts of the mind/body unit. If the mind/body and the soul are not co-existing in harmony, they are not at ease with each other and the situation is likely to lead to dis-ease, to disease. Either the mind or the body or both are affected.

Sense of identity

An important basis for a person's spiritual existence and well-being is a sense of identity. The eternal question 'Who am I?' is asked consciously or is part of the subconscious mind.

Philosophers went back a step further than this question, demanding absolute proof that 'I' exists. The French philosopher Descartes was satisfied with his finding which he expressed in Latin as '*Cogito, ergo sum.*' in English 'I think, therefore I am.' In this case the existence of the person is grounded within himself, proved by himself, to himself. This happens on a purely intellectual level, in the mind alone and will satisfy a philosopher.

The average person, however, is in a different position. He is not in the slightest doubt about his existence. He finds himself in tangible and compelling real-life situations which put the question about himself differently. It may be in the form of 'Am I somebody?' and 'Who am I?'

He derives his answer not so much from his own thinking, but from outside his own personal sphere, from the people around him, from the world around him and from the part he plays in this setting. The feedback he receives may not be positive at all, may not even be conclusive and not at all a basis for his spiritual existence and well-being. Only a spiritual source can give a valid answer. In the Bible we read that we are the children of our Heavenly Father, that He has called us by our name and therefore we are His. Because of this we know that we are somebody and we know who we are, no matter what happens. Our identity is unshakeable because we belong. We are never alone, never isolated.(1)

(1)   But now thus says the LORD, he who created you, O Jacob, he who formed you, O Israel: 'Fear not, for I have redeemed you; I have called you by name, you are mine.' (Isaiah 43:1)

God the Creator in the past, in the present and in the future

If we believe that God is the creator of heaven and earth, we must believe that He created man. He created man, not just man as we read about him in the Bible, but any man who has lived anywhere on this earth at any time. Whether we are followers of the theory of creation or the theory of evolution is, in our case, totally unimportant. If the Lord did not create man as we know him, then He definitely created the possibilities which were to develop into man as we know him. We can even say that man existed in the Will of the Lord even before he was created. And the Will of the Lord is the Will of our Almighty Father or even our Almighty Father Himself whose name is 'I am': without beginning, without end.

Archaeologists have found irrefutable evidence that some parts of the human body have changed since, let us say, the days of Java man and Peking man. As a result of this fact alone it cannot be doubted that God did not create man as he is today. We have to think, rather, that God created a being of certain physical, mental and spiritual characteristics at the beginning of the history of mankind. Quite obviously, he included in the make-up of this being the ability to develop, not just change, but develop according to His intentions and plans. This means quite clearly that the process of creation by the Lord was not restricted to a limited period of time in the past, but that it has continued from the beginning right up to the present day and will continue to the end of this world if He so decides.

The concept of creation is a total concept which forces us to believe that the Lord created everything in heaven and on earth. Furthermore, as already stated, He has been creating ever since the beginning as referred to in the Lord's prayer: 'Thy will be done, on earth as it is in heaven.' This is not just the acknowledgment by us of His absolute authority, but it is also the acknowledgment of the fact that His Will was at work not only within a limited period of initial creation, but that His Will has been done, is being done and will be done forever. Some people may like to think of God as the all-embracing energy, the all-pervading will at work in the whole universe.

The all-embracing Will of God

The concept of creation lays absolute claim to total acceptance. We either accept it without exception, or we totally reject it. Whatever our opinion or judgement of a limited period of time in history or of a specific historical event, whether we say it is good, whether we say it is bad - this opinion or judgement is overridden or overruled by the fact that whatever happens happens according to the Will of the Lord. He reigns supreme, He rules and, as someone put it: 'No matter what happens to you, remember that it had to go past the Lord first.'

This also applies to events which affect us one way or another and are not caused by actions of our fellow-men, such as natural catastrophes. Because everything which happens on this earth, even on the very personal level of each of us, has the Lord's approval, we have to attempt a very difficult step. We have to try and bring ourselves to realise that our definitions of good and bad are entirely relevant only to our own personal way of thinking, feeling and acting. In the wider perspective the concepts of good and bad are dissolved, are non-existent.

The ultimate statement would be that there is neither good nor bad, there is only the Will of God. It is easy to say this, it is easy to write this, it is easy to accept this if one is not in such difficulties that one cries out to the Lord from the depth.

If one cries out from the depth, then it is important to call on Him because Jesus knows the depth, He was there Himself. 'My God, my God, why hast thou forsaken me?' was His cry from the cross. (Mark 15:34).

The Will of God and man's freedom of choice

The fact that whatever happens represents the Will of God does not take away from us the freedom of personal choice, decision and initiative, nor does it absolve us from the responsibility for our attitudes and actions. On the other hand, what happens to us is beyond our control and we consider it to be the Will of God. What are God's guidelines for us? They are made known to us through His Word, the Scriptures, especially His Commandments. In addition to that He is also in direct communication with us, that is with the God in us, with our soul. In our soul there is His Light which we can allow to surround us and to be a lamp for our feet and a light to our path. (Psalm 119:105). He admonishes to stay within the light so that we remain children of the light.

What we do against the Will of the Lord is for us a transgression, a sin. If the consequence of such transgression affects another human being then, as soon as it enters his personal sphere, it becomes the Will of God for that human being. This to him will appear in the form of injury, sadness, loss, grief, injustice and whatever other forms the consequence of someone else's transgression may assume. The same principle works in reverse. Someone else's transgression will become for us the Will of God which can affect us in the guise of all sorts of afflictions.

And forgive us our trespasses as we forgive those who trespass against us

By taking the burden of our sins from us and dying for us on the cross, Christ has firmly located the process of forgiving within our lives here on earth. Christ died for the living and not for the dead. The act of His voluntary self-sacrifice is one of the manifestations of the Unconditional Love of our God. This unconditional love has set us free from the torment suffered by our soul, our mind and our body.

'And forgive us our trespasses' is a prayer that the Lord may have mercy on us. '. . . as we forgive those who trespass against us' is a pledge on our part which has the strength of an already accomplished fact.(1) Our transgressions and the transgressions of our fellow-men have been forgiven by God. Each individual has to follow on the human level and pass on the Unconditional Love of God to his fellow-man. To receive and to grant forgiveness is the Will of the Lord. This is the salvation which we have been promised and each one of us has an active role to play, each one of us is a worker in the Lord's vineyard here on earth.

It says in the Bible that those who believe in Christ and follow Him will be saved. To follow Him means to accept the Will of the Lord. It was the Will of the Lord that Christ suffered and died on the cross. He had not committed any sins, He died for the sins of others, for the sins of the whole of mankind. Our soul, the God in us, would grieve over our sins just as God our Father would grieve. The mind, knowing the Will of God, knows about sin. It is this knowledge which gives sin its reality, its life. It is this knowledge which establishes sin in the mind as a guilty conscience, as a tormentor of the mind. In turn, this tormentor uses the mind's line of communication to make its way into the body. From all of this, from sin itself and all the anguish and suffering it causes, Christ as the Son of God Almighty has set us free.(2)

(1) '. . . as we forgive those who trespass against us.'
The strength of an already accomplished fact which is implied in the above quotation is clearly expressed in the wording of some Bible translations. In the Revised Standard Version we read: 'and forgive us our debts, as we also have forgiven our debtors.' The French text is the equivalent of: 'forgive us our sins against you, as we ourselves have forgiven those who sinned against us.'
On the other hand, the German Bible based on Martin Luther's translation and the version 'Good News for Modern Man' express our commitment – similarly to the quotation in the text – as a general promise. (Matthew 6:12)
We wonder whether the translators, although presumably working with the same sources, had an option to translate either way. Or were some of them perhaps influenced by Matthew 5:23, 24? This passage tells the believer that, if he remembers that his brother has something against him when he is about to offer his gift at the altar, he should leave it in front of the altar. First he should go and be reconciled to his brother and only then should he return to make his offering.
Here we are shown that reconciliation with God is inseparable from reconciliation with one's fellow-man. Man's relationship with God is invariably the same as his relationship with his fellow-man because in each human being there is a portion of

the same God. And the God within us is the same God who is around us.

(2) In the days of the just God there was the concept that illness, disease and disability were punishment for sin.

The Lord sent a pestilence upon Israel as punishment for David's transgression. (2 Samuel 24:10-17)

When Jesus saw a blind man, His disciples asked Him, 'Rabbi, who sinned, this man or his parents that he was born blind?' (John 9:1,2)

In Matthew 9:1-8 we read that they brought a paralytic to Jesus. When Jesus saw their faith, He said to the paralytic, 'Take heart, my son; your sins are forgiven.'

God in the Old Testament

God and His teaching, as recorded in the Old Testament, represent a belief on a level appropriate to the people of those ages. The basis of this belief is formulated in the covenant the Lord made with His chosen people. It is God who takes the initiative, proposing His covenant which offers promises to His chosen people, but also imposes obligations on them. The covenant with Abraham is found in 1 Moses:17, the one with the people of Israel led by Moses is in 2 Moses:19-24. The latter contains the Ten Commandments and further detailed instructions. The five Books of Moses as a whole are known as the Law. One of the striking features of that era is the fact that He was the Invisible God and the Unapproachable God. Just to see Him meant certain death. (2 Moses 19:12, 13, 21-24).

God in the New Testament

The Christian faith as we know it today must be considered to be on a higher level than the belief system of the Old Testament. This new covenant, already foreshadowed by some prophets of the Old Testament (e.g. Jeremiah 31:31-34), is fulfilled by Christ as recorded in the New Testament. Jesus became the founder of the new covenant which is between God and His new people which embraces all peoples of the world (1 Corinthians 11:25). God came to live among His people, His Son sacrificed Himself for His people.

Jesus said that He had not come to destroy the Law, but to fulfil it, thus emphasising continuity between the beliefs of the Old Testament and the New Testament. Instead of continuity one might call it development, growth. The Old Testament literally cried out for a new and different covenant according to which the Lord would put His Law within the people, would write it on their hearts and they were all to know Him, from the least of them to the greatest – through the God in us, our soul – (Jeremiah 31:31-34). Could we not say that the Old Testament is the first stage and the New Testament is the second stage?

The individual, his belief and the church

Sometimes people may feel that religious belief systems are so forceful in their demands and so dogmatic in their formulation that they deprive a person of his individual power and of the freedom to make his own decisions. The church as the worldly representative of religious beliefs may therefore appear in the same light.

It must be said at the beginning of our deliberations that the church as an institution feels called upon to derive from the belief as such certain interpretations and conclusions which become first guidelines, then possibly strict regulations and then possibly even part of the belief itself. To what extent a member of a church feels compelled to go beyond the spirit of his faith, and adhere to the letter of the guidelines and possibly even believe in the letter of the strict regulations – this is entirely a matter for the individual to decide.

When the church lays down a dogma it is bound by this action to enforce it. This provides the vast majority of its members with the wonderful security of peace of mind and soul which is the essence of pastoral care. This is the ideal situation for those who are happy to be taken care of in this way.

The disadvantage of this situation is that not everybody is happy to be taken care of in this way. Instead of the feeling of security, instead of the absence of doubt and query some believers feel this to be restrictive. They may feel that to be told what to believe and what not to believe is the result of an agreement by the governing body of their church. For them this excludes their personal search for truth because questions of an individual nature may put them at variance with some aspects of the teaching of their church. They find themselves deprived of direct access to God of which each believer has been assured by Christ's word 'I am the way, and the truth, and the life; no one comes to the Father, but by me.' (John 14:6).

This situation does not only preclude access to God for the believer, but it also 'restricts' God's access to the believer or makes it sometimes 'officially illegal' if it may be put this way. If God communicates with the believer in messages which are compatible with the established doctrine of the church, there are no complications. If God's communication encourages or even tells a believer to take steps which lead him outside the approved area of his faith, then the situation is similar to what the reformers of the past experienced. Not only the reformers of the past. Those of the present and of the future will not be able to avoid this problem.

A long line of reformers paid with their lives for their convictions which, in many cases, were the ground-work for the formation of churches which are now recognised members of the broad spectrum of Christian denominations.

The significance of the word 'religion'

It may be helpful to look at the meaning of the word 'religion'. There are at least two opinions regarding the original basic meaning of this word. One opinion suggests that the word, in Latin, meant 'reverence for the gods, fear of God, religious awe, consciousness of wrong, religious scruple', coming from the Latin verb *relegere* which, among other things means 'to ponder over, to give heed to, observe, care for'. Some writers on ancient Latin suggest that it comes from the verb *religare* which is 'to bind', connecting it with the idea of 'a binding, an obligation'.(1) Whichever opinion one accepts is only of linguistic importance. One interpretation suggests straight-out 'binding, obligation' and in the other one 'fear of God', for instance, will certainly lead to a sense of obligation and commitment.

(1)   *The Universal Dictionary of the English Language.*

The believer as a member of a church

When someone joins a religious organisation, especially when this organisation has already developed into a fully-grown church, he will be faced with a complex situation. While previously his belief was the beginning and the end of his faith, he finds now that his belief is the focal point of a body of people and certain administrative structures. We may liken this to the birth of a human being: the soul enters a body, it is a form of incarnation. Alas, this word 'incarnation' comes from the Latin word for 'flesh' and the process foreshadows the eternal polarisation of 'the spirit is willing, but the flesh is weak'. Because the church as an organisation sees itself as a vessel which contains the Holy Spirit it is inspired to develop its worldly, physical aspect by following and obeying certain rules which govern a worldly, physical existence. These worldly, physical requirements must be met in order to secure the survival of the organisation. Quite rightly, the church can claim that it is a vessel which contains the Holy Spirit and the word 'contain' originally meant 'to hold together'. The church consists of a number of persons whose souls are in themselves a manifestation of the Holy Spirit. The church is the place where the Word of God is kept in writing and where it is preached. It is the venue where its members come to hear the Word of God, to study it, to have it explained and to enjoy the fellowship of their fellow-believers, just to name some aspects of a church.

It is a very delicate balance, the balance between the spiritual function and the physical function of the church. The spiritual function derives its primary inspiration and guidance from the Bible which is the Word of God as we know it. There are differences of opinion whether the Bible as we know it is the complete Word of God as revealed to man and whether what we find in the Bible today is the exact Word of God as revealed to man. In order to lay down guidelines, in order to clarify the situation and to make it possible for its members to practise a secure faith, the church formulates a doctrine. This doctrine in effect freezes the Word of God as it was written and to the extent we know it today. This process fixes the Word of God once and for all which actually means that God has not spoken for about 1900 years. If He has spoken, His Word was either not heard or it was ignored, or it was, after earnest thought and deliberation, not considered compatible with the Bible as we know it or with the doctrine of a particular church.

There is, however, sufficient room for some individual members of a church to have their own personal faith which is not identical with the faith proclaimed according to the doctrine of their church. They may continue to be members of that church - fully aware of their situation - without being hypocritical or condescending. On the other hand, there are people who feel so strongly that they will not participate any further in the life of their church, will not consider it to be their church any more. The believers can find themselves in a dilemma, convinced that there is only one God, that this God would speak to us only in one way, in His Way, being consistent also in what He tells us and yet - there are so many different churches professing not always the same Christian faith in detail. The only way out may be the thought and the decision: 'This is the right church for me,' or 'I will go to another church,' or 'I will go it alone.'

The worldly function of the church is primarily to assure its physical existence now and in the future. It becomes a tool which is used by its leaders for this purpose. The method chosen may be inspired by the Scriptures, or, at the other end of the scale, it may be inspired by cold-blooded business considerations. Between these two extremes there would be an endless number of variations and combinations possible.

Some members of a congregation as well as some outsiders will feel that the worldly affairs of a particular church are run in such a way that they are obviously not governed and guided by religious principles. Again, individual members of that church may find that they can, quite honestly, participate in the life of that church, perhaps in the hope that they may be able to rectify the situation. Or they may decide to leave that church.

One is strongly tempted to say that it is a great pity that the world is as it is. There is a very apt picture in Greek mythology: the soul rides through the sky in a chariot drawn by two horses, a black one and a white one. The white one represents good, it pulls upwards. The black one represents evil, it pulls downwards. Perhaps this picture has universal validity, for our entire world, including our churches. The Lord has assured us that His Kingdom is not of this world, but that one day He will return to establish it here amongst us.

Before the Lord, human wisdom is but foolishness

We read in the Bible that the fool says in his heart that there is no God.(1) The fool may not be a fool by our human level of intelligence. This person may be highly intelligent, may have a keen sense of fairness and justice, may be an astute observer, but, in spite of it all, may come to the conclusion that there is no God. What is more, he may be able to back up all his findings with solid arguments. Yet, before the Lord all human intelligence and knowledge are but foolishness.

Why is it then that this non-believer can fend off any ideas which do not fit into his system and why can he do so apparently in a logical manner? It is because harmonious interaction of a sufficiently large number of ideas and concepts creates an organism which makes a concerted effort to live, and to live through all kinds of situations. In its pursuit of development and survival this system will build its own structure, its own method of functioning, it will spawn new ideas and concepts 'according to its kind', it will purge itself, it will attempt to keep itself strong and healthy. Anything which endangers this process within will be eliminated and justifiably so - in the interest of the all-embracing system. Anything which approaches this system from without will be quickly assessed as compatible or incompatible, as friend or foe. A powerful immune mechanism operating on the intellectual level of the non-believer and his agnostic system attacks and destroys or rejects any idea which presents danger.

It may be added here that the same kind of principle ultimately applies to many systems and organisations be they in the economic world, the political field and also in areas of intellectual and religious activities.

(1)   Psalm 53:1

Resurrection of the body

In Matthew 22 we read that the Sadducees asked Christ which one of the several men a woman was married to here on earth would be her husband in the hereafter. Christ answered them: 'You are wrong, because you know neither the scriptures nor the power of God. For in the resurrection they neither marry nor are given in marriage, but are like angels in heaven.' (Verses 29, 30). Similar information is given in Luke 20:35, 36 where it says that they 'neither marry nor are given in marriage, for they cannot die any more, because they are equal to angels and are sons of God, being sons of the resurrection'. This means that in the hereafter, in eternal life, the person is a new creation beyond our understanding. He is a new creation of soul, mind and body of purely spiritual qualities, like angels.

Man is born a sinner

That man is born a sinner is not a judgement, not a condemnation, but a pure statement of fact. Soul, mind and body are bound to travel the road of life together, they are the personification of the frailty of human nature. There is no point in fighting against that because any success of such an undertaking will only be relative and temporary. The only way to peace and happiness is complete surrender and subsequent acceptance. Joyful acceptance it can be and it must be. Our soul, the God in us, is there and will always be there, out-lasting mind and body even though their noise and clamour may drown out its divine voice. To have faith in this soul which is part of our Father in Heaven is not only to have faith in God, but also to have faith in oneself. Our faith combined with God's Unconditional Love is the wonderful result of our surrender and acceptance and the gratifying benefit of receiving the Lord.

'Love your enemies' really means 'Love your neighbours'

God asks us to love our enemies. Is it possible that He asks us to do so as an exercise for our soul to use its inherent goodness, to find an application for its essential kindness, to demonstrate one of the guidelines of its divine nature? Does He demand from this God within us unconditional love as an achievable act? Or does He merely wish to point us in the direction of an unachievable goal, knowing that in this world we will – as the combination of soul, mind and body – quite often not be able to go the full distance? Will He expect us to go only part of the way towards unconditional forgiveness, accepting our endeavour and our attempts already as 'something worthwhile'?

If love towards our enemies were only of concern for our soul, then our soul, the God in us, would not have to overcome any obstacles within our personality. However, this God within us is not alone. There is our mind and there is our body. Would not the mind immediately voice its opposition, saying that it is against all sound reasoning to completely disregard a painful experience which has established our enemy as someone who has made life very difficult for us, has caused us suffering of varying degrees, or has even been a threat to our very existence? Would not the body join in this train of thought, drawing attention to the adverse effects which disappointment, deceived trust, sorrow, anger, fear, anguish and dismay have had on its well-being? Would not the body sometimes be able to literally show proof of its physical injuries for all to see?

To some degree we all have suffered because of the action of other people. The word 'action' would have the widest possible meaning, the word 'activity' offers itself as a more adequate term. It could have been a deliberate set of steps taken by someone. It could have been quite inadvertent and not in keeping with the person's character. It could have been the result of a person's desperate struggle for survival. However, these various aspects would not make any difference to the ultimate effect these activities have.

The last paragraph could be re-written, beginning like this: 'To some degree all our fellow-men have suffered because of the actions of us, their fellow-men.' We could say then that our enemies are really our neighbours and we, their enemies, are really their neighbours. We are asked to love our neighbours as we love ourselves. In turn, our fellow-men are asked to love us, their neighbours, as they love themselves. Therefore, 'Love your neighbour' is the all embracing commandment which includes the 'Love your enemies' request.

You shall love your neighbour as yourself

The word 'love' has various meanings in English according to the circumstances it refers to. In the days of Christ there were two words in the Greek language for 'love': 'agape' and 'eros'. The word 'eros' expresses the love between man and woman, referring foremost to the physical relationship. Naturally, the bond between husband and wife would go beyond that, including a spiritual element. In the attitude expressed by 'agape' we find a spiritual basis for various specific aspects, such as sympathy, caring and sharing, concern and empathy. The love for one's neighbour or fellow-man is expressed in German in just one word, 'Nächstenliebe'.

The demand that you love your neighbour as you love yourself may sound very general, rather vague and quite abstract. For that reason it invites a closer look. The words 'you love yourself' express a very positive attitude like saying 'yes' to your life. They express first and foremost the paramount desire, determination and practical effort to survive. Unknowingly, you grant yourself the right to survival and you pursue it vigorously. Once this basic need has been satisfied, additional expectations and entitlements then receive your attention. According to the kind of society, cultural surroundings and economic climate you live in these aspects may in due course assume the importance and recognition of fundamental rights.

The awareness of your own basic needs and additional requirements of physical, social and spiritual nature can obviously make it easier for you to have the right attitude to your fellow-man. As you go through life trying to make it an enjoyable and rewarding experience which is not only acceptable in the eyes of the Lord, but is also considered positive by your fellow-man – so does your neighbour want to lead his life. As you place no ifs and buts on your own attitude to yourself and to your goals in life, as you see no need to justify your way of life to yourself – so shall your attitude be to your fellow-man also. As your love for yourself is without condition so shall your love for your fellow-man also be without condition.

'You shall love your neighbour as you love yourself' is the request for unconditional love.

The cross: symbol of faith and of man's relationships

It has been said that the cross must also be considered to be the symbol of man's relationships, not only the symbol of faith. The horizontal line signifies the relationship between man and his fellow-man. The vertical line signifies the relationship between God and man. For our considerations the very significant part of the cross is the point where both lines intersect. We may and we must call this the 'crucial' point – 'crucial' being derived from the Latin word 'crux', meaning 'cross'. At this point the relationship between man and his fellow-man is identical with the relationship between God and man. When we are asked to love our enemies we are asked to show unconditional love to our fellow-man. This request is directed from our Almighty Father in Heaven not to our body, not to our mind, but to our soul. This request is directed from God Almighty in Heaven to God in our soul. The request for unconditional love is the Will of God and the Will of God is God Himself. God is Unconditional Love.

The concept of 'good' and 'bad'

It has already been stated that the notions of good and bad, of right and wrong, of just and unjust and other diametrically opposed concepts suit our way of thinking.

When we want to help somebody to understand the meaning of the word 'sad', for instance, or when we want to give a definition of it we tend to reach automatically for the quick solution, the opposite. We may then simply say: 'One is sad when one is not at all happy.' Diametrically opposed concepts are a very important part of our thinking process. This is one of the reasons why the use of opposites is an essential ingredient of our religious thinking.

These opposites play an important part in our non-physical life because they are such an obvious part of our everyday real-life experience. We are surrounded by combinations such as right and left, top and bottom, flat and hilly, light and dark, night and day, light and heavy, quickly and slowly. They are a very important principle of our physical world. From our physical perceptions we move into the metaphysical areas, taking with us the tools of thinking which we acquired beforehand.

Certainly, each concept, each thought and each word has a self-contained meaning in its own right. One can give a description of the concept of 'good' without using the concept of its opposite, the word 'bad'. This one-way statement that 'good' is such and such can be reinforced if it is so desired, made stronger, more vivid, more impressive by the addition that 'good' is not this and that.

There has to be what we in our terminology call 'good' and 'bad'. There has to be also the full range of transitional values to fill the space between these two opposites. Why? It is the basis for our freedom of choice. It allows us to exercise our will. Both these conditions are essential for us to be what we are: masters within us of our destiny. Freedom, authority, dignity are within. They are granted us by our Creator and because of this fact they must be recognised as the Will of God. How we use these gifts is entirely our own decision. Whether we use them for purposes which 'find favour in the eyes of the Lord' or not is our very personal decision.

Has God spoken His final Word to us?

There cannot be such a thing as the final Word of God to us. The words we know, the words of our language and languages as such have a limited time span of maximum performance. To put it differently; the words we use are our own words, we can handle their pronunciation, their spelling and the meaning they convey.

Languages have evolved as a natural process alongside the evolvement of our abilities and patterns of thinking, feeling and acting. For this reason, the Bible as we know it today would not have meant anything to

Stone Age man. His metaphysical experience had to be within the capabilities of the spoken word because man thinks in words - silent or spoken. Conversely, words spoken by the Lord to Stone Age man in his language would not be meaningful to us today.

Different cults and forms of worship

To come back to the metaphysical experience, let us say, of Stone Age man. *If* God revealed Himself to man in those times, it would have had to be in a way commensurate with the capability of man as he was at that time. We must also put it another way. *When* God revealed Himself to man in those times, it had to be commensurate with the capabilities of man as he was at that time. We have to make this statement in two different forms because we are not to say what God did, or what God did not do. We must not succumb to the temptation to funnel and filter God's Will and God's Actions through our human brain and declare what God's Will is and what it is not, what He created and what He did not create. Furthermore, we must not extend judgement another step by decreeing that whatever we do not deem to be God's work must be the work of Satan. These thoughts make it improper for us to judge the early forms of worship of the sun, the earth and other parts of the Lord's Creation. These thoughts should also prevent us from judging the early forms of worship and condemning them as heathen because God may have favourably accepted these religious practices. We err fundamentally if we raise ourselves to the status of defenders of the Lord whether we concern ourselves with something which happened in the past or something which is happening now.

There is the important question of offerings to the Lord. In the Old Testament we read of various offerings such as cereal offerings and animal offerings. The offerings were to be valuable enough and important enough to the worshipper to be adequate expression of his gratitude, his requests and his veneration. The dedication ceremony of the Temple of Jerusalem illustrates this point.(1) The offering of life to please God or any deity has often been regarded as the most valuable kind of offering. In the Old Testament it was the lives of animals. In other cultures not only animals were sacrificed, but also human beings. These human sacrifices ranged from prisoners to slaves to members of the same people. Some of the latter were sacrificed against their will, others were sacrificed not because they volunteered, but they still accepted it as their duty or destiny. It has been stated that on some occasions in the Inca culture sacrifices of the best warriors were required. These warriors volunteered and by doing so not only performed a personal act of worship, but also brought great honour on their families and the districts they came from. It has also been stated that in these cases the men were drugged so that there was no pain.

We must also bear in mind that with pre-Christian religious rites the risk already existed that human motives and scheming infiltrated what once were pure religious practices.

(1) King Solomon offered as a sacrifice twenty-two thousand oxen and a hundred and twenty thousand sheep. So the king and all the people dedicated the house of God. (2 Chronicles 7:5)

In defence of God, His Word and His church

Since the establishment of the Christian church there have been no human sacrifices, naturally. However, there have been human beings killed in the defence of the Lord, in defence of His Word and in defence of His church. There is a long list of reformers or their followers who were executed such as J. Hooper, W. Tyndale, H. Latimer and N. Ridley, just to mention a few English names. A notable example of a different type of person and of a different case is Joan of Arc who was burnt at the stake in Rouen, France, in 1431 after having been found guilty by a church tribunal. The same Joan of Arc was then beatified in 1909 and declared a Saint in 1920.

Large numbers lost their lives during the Inquisition and religious wars. It must be remembered that in religious wars all kinds of motives and goals which have nothing to do with religion become involved in the planning and execution of hostilities. Of course, the victims were not sacrificed during religious ceremonies as expressions of gratitude and allegiance to the Lord by those responsible for their deaths. In an indirect way, however, they lost their lives at least partly because of the endeavour of certain people to defend the Lord, His Word and His church, as a demonstration of their faith, their devotion and to please the Lord.

Some of these people responsible for the deaths 'in the defence of God' may have genuinely believed that their actions were guided by divine inspiration. However, when Christians clash and the confrontation ends in suffering and bloodshed then one cannot believe that both parties are completely guided by divine inspiration. At least some of the hostility is in the name of a belief system which contains a strong human element.

Churches established since the Reformation, it appears, cannot avoid 'defending the Word of the Lord' in our days either. Of course, nobody is burnt at the stake any more, but in 1992 a Dr. Peter Cameron, Principal of St. Andrew's College of the University of Sydney, was charged by his church on two counts of making statements in a public sermon inconsistent with the Westminster Confession of Faith (a statement on the authority of the Bible).

Christ foreshadowed antagonism and persecution with this warning to His disciples: 'They will put you out of the synagogues; indeed, the hour is coming when whoever kills you will think he is offering service to God.' (John 16:2).

The combination of spiritual and worldly powers

In the existence side by side of spiritual and worldly powers the ideal situation would be that the worldly power would be guided by the spiritual power. However, some representatives of spiritual power are known to have assumed worldly functions to pursue worldly goals. This can even go so far as to lead to the creation of states in which the only law is a particular religion, or, more appropriately put, its interpretation according to human judgement and sometimes even for the sake of expediency.

And His Word became . . .

When Christ presented His teaching in parables, His Word became pictures. It became pictures taken from every-day life of the people around Him and, endowed with a spiritual meaning, these pictures were put back into people's everyday lives.

When the Lord Almighty sent His Son into our world, His Word became flesh. God revealed Himself to mankind as a human being and, as Jesus Christ, He put Himself into people's everyday lives. Jesus offered, yes, literally offered to those around Him the full range of possibilities a human being can encounter in his lifetime: He was admired and despised, revered and cursed, cherished and persecuted,

43

exalted and humiliated; though innocent, He was found guilty and put to death. Three days after His death He again entered the everyday life of His chosen people, again as God revealed to mankind. He appeared as the personification of life after death, more than personification: to His followers He was life after death, so real, so convincing that Thomas could touch Him. One might even go so far as to say that Christ played the ultimate role of the parable of God the Almighty, where the word became flesh.

The unlimited Presence of God

From the belief that God has given each human being a soul as part of Himself we may conclude that God, if He so wished, had given part of Himself to the rest of His Creation. Since God need not necessarily be what we are able to perceive Him to be, the extent to which 'He breathed His Breath' into the rest of His Creation we cannot know. How His Spirit, which is, or at least can be in all His Creation in addition to being in man, manifests itself is also not for us to determine.

In the past the Lord chose to reveal Himself, no doubt He does it right now somewhere and somehow and no doubt He will continue to do so in the future. Since the Lord has said of Himself 'I am', our concept of past, present and future and of time in general is only 'our way' and not 'His Way'. The second concept which governs our physical existence is space and again it is of no relevance to the Lord. He said that 'where two or three are gathered in my name, there am I in the midst of them.' (Matthew 18:20). Not only is the Lord constantly 'within' each one of us, but He is also 'between and among' us.

God reveals Himself to us. He comes to us. It is not for us to put Him into anything which is alive or not alive. This is the fundamental difference between worship of God and idolatry.

God reveals Himself whenever and however He wishes. Because of this He is not just our Lord, He is also the Lord of all Creation at all times. He is the Lord and 'I am' is one of His names.

What is being said can be upsetting to a person who is an honest, sincere and devoted Christian and whose spiritual life has been proceeding according to the teachings of his particular denomination. The word 'Christian' in itself conveys to many faithful, consciously or subconsciously, the notion that 'faith in God was started about 2000 years ago'. When one then is reminded of the Old Testament one hastens to modify this opinion to 'the real and correct faith in God was started about 2000 years ago'.

Faith in God

Faith in God, being based completely on God's revelation to His faithful, is commensurate with this revelation. This revelation determines in every detail what his faith in Him shall be: the symbols which convey His Godhead, the way the faithful are to worship. In other words, His revelation gives to the human being a transposition of His Will into the range of perception of this human being, into the concepts within his mental and spiritual capacity. The fact is this: the Lord who is without beginning and without end revealed Himself in His Way to man prior to what records we have of Him and differently to the records we have if and when He chose to do so. To use the Bible as we know it to argue against such a kind of revelation, which is outside our own religious experience, is futile. The Bible reveals God in terms of our human language and mental and spiritual capacity. To understand God as He is we would have to be exactly like Him. To argue against the Bible is equally futile for someone to whom God revealed Himself in a different way, because He chose to do so. These two kinds of arguments would simply mean that we tell the Lord what we accept as His Will and what we do not. It goes even further than that, we tell the Lord what He created and what He did not. Ultimately, we tell the Lord what we allow Him to be and what we do not. And all this possibly because of our religious zeal. Were not the Jews all set to stone Christ for blasphemy? In John 10:31-33 we read: 'The Jews took up stones again to stone him. Jesus answered them, "I have shown you many good works from the Father: for which of these do you stone me?" The Jews answered him, "We stone you for no good work but for blasphemy; because you, being a man, make yourself God." '

Pre-Christian religions

It is not appropriate to look at the ritual of pre-Christian religions from our own and present point of view. It is especially not appropriate to compare the pre-Christian ceremonial with our own religious ceremonial because a comparison is frequently an irresistible temptation to consider us to be on a more advanced level of spiritual experience. Our thoughts do not even stop there because they must run their full course. Because

45

our religious belief demands absolute acceptance, it is implied - to our way of thinking - that our belief lays claim to being the only valid belief. Indeed, the Lord says: 'You shall have no other gods before me.' (2 Moses 20:3).

For the pre-Christian worshippers each ceremonial object and each ceremonial movement had symbolic meaning. For them they were symbols which evoked the spirits, which brought the spirits into their human presence. It is impossible for us to experience the same religious feeling when considering these symbols unless we completely abandon our present religious stance. Their religious experience connected with their rituals was inspired by the spirits they knew. Our religious experience connected with our rituals is inspired by the spirits or the Spirit which we know. It is not the ritual which is the criterion, it is the spiritual experience.

The word 'pantheism' makes itself heard. This word by itself is only a combination of letters and does not come to life until we give it its meaning, or better, meanings. There is the type of pantheism which is based on the idea that each animal, plant and inanimate object is the home of some spirit. These spirits are often either male or female to fit in with our human experience. They are identical with what they dwell in. For instance, a tree spirit cannot live in a river. Whether the Lord decided to reveal Himself in this way and in a specific era is not important knowledge. What is important, however, is the knowledge that the existence of these spirits meets man's needs to look up to something in awe. Our inner being has to have this kind of balance to the same extent as our body has to have the right atmospheric pressure around it to prevent the inherent energy from blowing itself apart. Because the sight or the idea of somebody worshipping in front of a tree is not within the range of our spiritual experience, we compensate for this lack of experience using a deft mental move: we judge. In such an incomprehensible set of circumstances our judgement has to produce an unfavourable finding in order to respect and preserve the integrity of our world of ideas. Because we do not realise, or we do not wish to realise, that the person in front of the tree is worshipping a spirit which could in fact be the kind of revelation chosen by God, our perception is that the person is worshipping a spirit which cannot be a creation of God and is therefore a satanic spirit. Our integrity is intact, we are completely in command, the world is as we know it is and we feel duty-bound to make this fact known.

God's Creation is holy in detail and in its sum total

God created not only man, but also the heavens and the earth. Man for this reason is holy and although God has set him over the world around him, man must still respect the world around him for what it is: the Lord's Creation and as such holy. Man is only a steward, he does not own anything, he enters this world with nothing and he leaves this world with nothing. It is more to the point to say that his soul enters this world clothed in a body and his soul leaves this world just by itself, naked, even with less than it arrived.

The acceptance that the world around us is animated by the Spirit of the Lord and therefore sanctified may immediately be decried and derided by some. It may even be branded as blasphemous as it may be considered to be a kind of pantheism which would question the principle that there is only one God. Of course, there is only one God, but He can be everywhere at once if He wishes. We have heard that 'The earth is the LORD's and the fulness thereof, the world and those who dwell therein.' (Psalm 24:1).

Why is the world the Lord's? Is it the Lord's because we acknowledge Him as the ruler, or we acknowledge Him as the Creator whose Will is embodied in every single aspect of His Creation? A daunting question for us all who have been consuming the Lord's Creation instead of working in harmony within it since we are part of it. It is more a question to us than to previous generations because we know more in this respect than they did. We have a clear knowledge of what we should do and should not do. It is the knowledge about right and wrong which changes the action from a merely undesirable and inappropriate one to a sin.

Making decisions

When we make a decision and choose accordingly we can take into account the situation our choice refers to. If this is our only consideration we are entirely at the mercy of this situation. Its changes will vindicate or condemn our choice: at one change we may be proved right, at the next change we may be proved wrong.

This state of affairs clearly points to the need that a guiding principle higher than the situation in question has to be involved and be the deciding factor. Because this higher principle can be found only within a person, the facts are very clear: freedom of choice rests within the person. In fact, freedom of any kind can be found only within a person.

The Lord's constant Presence is our salvation

The Lord is with us constantly till the end of the world. He is present not as an onlooker, not as a benevolent spectator, but He is present as His Divine Will. This Divine Will is constantly at work, in us and around us. It manifests itself in various ways, one of them being, what we call, our salvation.

When we stumble, the Lord steadies us; when we fall, He lifts us up. He does it in His own Way and He does it in His own time. To us it may at times be unnoticeable, it may again seem that His help takes such a long time to reach us, it may even appear that He does not help us at all – that He has turned away from us, that He has forsaken us. Our salvation is part of His Will. Because His Will is ever present, our salvation is ever present. It is here, right now, in our lifetime here on earth. He makes the first move, He endlessly repeats His first move, in every moment in our lives there is the pulse of His first move.

It has been said that in every moment of life there is a moment of death. In each moment of our lives the energy of life is stronger than the energy of death till the balance tips the other way. Death affects only the mind/body, not the soul. The word 'death' is best replaced by the word 'transition'. Not because we gloss over an unpleasant reality, no, but we have to see the situation as it is.

The end of our earthly life is but the beginning of our eternal life. We pass over from one life to the next. The Lord Jesus Christ has shown us. His supreme sacrifice on the cross and His subsequent resurrection are the living proof that eternal life is ours. This proof and assurance is indeed the most wonderful feature of our salvation. In every moment in our lives here on earth there is the pulse of His first move of Love. In the last moment of our lives here on earth there is nothing but His Divine Will and His Fatherly Love which carry us across into eternal life. All we have to do is allow His Divine Will to take its course, allow us to be guided, helped and blessed. Here and now. In this life and in the next. Till the end of the world.(1)

> (1)   . . . I am with you always, to the close of the age. (Matthew 28:20)

Various ways of entering faith

There has always been the question whether the ability to believe, the readiness to be open and receptive to the Grace and Mercy of our Heavenly Father - whether all this is, can be and must be the result of our human effort or whether it is God-given.

When we look at the conversion of Saul on the road to Damascus which changed him from Saul the persecutor into Paul the apostle, we can say that it was a dramatic act on the part of God. In this case the Lord practically smote Saul and resurrected him as Paul. Naturally, not every conversion against the will of the person concerned need be as dramatic as Paul's.

There is also a way of opening oneself to the word of God as a completely voluntary act. The development leading to this decision may take place in the subconscious area of the person so that the decision itself is like the opening of a flower, only the final stage of the development becomes visible.

For someone else it may mean a progression from one stage to the next of a clear thought process. This may indeed require a complete restructuring of one's inner personality which necessitates as a starting point an assessment of one's self. Of one's self on its own and of one's self in relationship to whatever surrounds this self. The first move may be to step down from one's vantage-point, to become one of the other beings without having to reduce one's sense of identity, one's self-respect and one's wholeness. This change will require, amongst other things, a strong feeling of humility, of acknowledgment of the existence - the equally justified and absolutely necessary existence - of everybody and everything around us. Whereas one's starting point was the vantage-point of self-justification on the basis of values and judgement, one has now arrived at a stage where there is no judgement, but only unconditional acceptance. This unconditional acceptance may be on the basis of clear logic alone, or it may also be pervaded by an ever-increasing appreciation, respect and love, resulting in a sense of belonging, of comfort and of fellowship.

This fundamental change can be likened to the discovery of Copernicus who made the revolutionary observation that the sun and many stars do not revolve around the earth. These stars, including the earth, revolve around the sun. The same set of circumstances applies to the human being: man is not a pivotal point for the world around him.

Instead, one's ego is part of the vast array of the Lord's Creation which revolves around the Lord. This acknowledgment is the surrender of the ego and its absolute authority to the Lord who then reciprocates in the spirit of His Unconditional Love: He gives us a new ego, a new identity, the identity of one of His children. He says: 'Fear not, for I have redeemed you; I have called you by name, you are mine.' (Isaiah 43:1).

There are and always have been questions in this context. If the Lord does not change a person into a believer against that person's will and if He does not grant a person the decision to become a believer, what then? Is it not God who makes it possible for somebody to open himself to His Word? If somebody is not given the opportunity or the ability to receive the Word of God, is that not a refusal by the Lord? Does the Lord exclude some people from the gracious gift of His faith and if so, why?

These questions have to be asked in sincerity and humility. It is possible for a believer to have questions and to express them because it is acceptable to the Lord that our understanding of His Will just cannot go beyond the limitations of our human nature. There can be a vast difference between the deliberation of questions like these as religious theory in general and the validity of questions of this nature when they apply to the practical situation involving a specific person in particular. What we, at one stage, consider to be the Will of God need not necessarily be an unchangeable Will of God for ever. Because He hears our prayers, because He listens to us, because He is merciful, we can obtain His gift of faith through our prayers.

About praying

Some people feel that they cannot pray. There is nothing special about praying which makes it different from speaking or thinking. Anybody who has that ability can pray, pray aloud or silently in his thoughts. We can speak to the Lord, we can talk with Him as we would with anyone we know, such as members of our family, friends or acquaintances. We can be completely open, completely frank, completely without hesitation. He will always hear and He will always listen. Furthermore, He is not in the far distance, He is right next to us, He is even right within us, in our soul. He will always understand. He already knows why we come to Him before we even formulate our thoughts. That is why we can be so absolutely honest with Him, as honest as with ourselves. In fact, it is easier to be honest with the Lord than with oneself. All this is a wonderful experience because it allows us to cast our burden upon the Lord. We have Him as our friend who forgives us whenever we ask His forgiveness, simply by talking with Him and by asking. It may take a long time, it may even be only towards the end of our life here on earth that we become fully aware of the extent of our faith. If even towards our final moments we feel that we have not been granted what we so earnestly wished and prayed for, we can always be completely sure; the Lord hears our prayer. The Lord always hears our prayer, especially in times of agonising doubt. He is quite familiar with the following words which we may repeat as Martin Luther did: 'I believe; help my unbelief!' (Mark 9:24).

The fact alone that we pray is proof that we acknowledge Him as our Lord. That in itself is an act of faith and we will be saved by our faith and the Grace of our Lord. As long and as soon as we pray we are believers.

The Spirit and our worship of the Spirit

The Spirit was before the name. We needed the name and therefore the Spirit assumed a name. We needed a certain way to worship the Spirit and therefore the Spirit told us how to worship It. We needed to know about the Spirit and therefore the Spirit revealed Itself to us.

As the Spirit has assumed various names and revealed Itself in various ways in various parts of the world and at various times in the history of mankind, we have lost sight of the Oneness of the Spirit. Our various names for It, our various rituals to worship It and our various doctrines have come between It and us.

Because we identify It with names, rituals and doctrines, we run the risk of making It identical with name, ritual and doctrine. This leads to the situation where the Spirit comes under our influence: we think, we discuss, we write, we teach, we stipulate, we declare an acceptable doctrine - we make It our Spirit. It is certainly true that It wants to be our Spirit, but not our Spirit in our image.

This pattern of development appears to be of necessity to our human nature, it creates a common ground between the Spirit and us. We must be aware of this, we must acknowledge its existence and its nature. We must furthermore accept that from this pattern of development arises the need for change, for a re-birth, for a re-formation whenever the forces of change gain enough momentum.

The word 're-formation' or 'reformation' conveys precisely what is involved or should be involved. The content is not affected, only the form in which this content is presented is altered. The content is ultimately the Spirit and the form is the ways and means which we need in order to have access to the Spirit.

There is only one element in our spiritual life which does not change: it existed already before it came into being, it has no beginning and no end, there is no past and no future, there is only the everlasting presence. It is the Spirit and Its Name is 'I am'.

The Holy Trinity

For many of us the Holy Trinity can be an elusive concept. To put it briefly: it is Three in One and One in Three at the same time. God the Father is in God the Son Jesus and both are in the Holy Ghost. In reverse it is the Holy Ghost at the same time in God the Son Jesus and in God the Father.

This attempt at defining the Holy Trinity sounds and indeed is rather futile, quite inadequate and actually cannot convey an understanding of the Holy Trinity. The Holy Trinity is simply beyond our logical understanding. The mind is not equipped to grasp its nature. The heart, or more appropriately, the soul, has a vision, has indefinable thoughts not of the nature of the Holy Trinity, but of Its Presence. This is the only way our soul relates and can relate to the Holy Trinity: be aware of Its Presence. The words ' vision, indefinable thoughts' prove to be totally unsuitable terms in comparison with the word ' awareness' . Our awareness of the Holy Trinity is the sum total of our perception of the Holy Trinity. It is the sum total of the human ability regarding the Holy Trinity.

Therefore it has not been man who has been investigating God and has arrived at the definition 'the Holy Trinity'. It was again God who took the initiative by revealing Himself to man in terms of man's thoughts and words. First God became the Father then, with Christ, God became the Son, but He has always been the Holy Ghost. One may be permitted to say that the Spirit revealed Himself to man as God the Father, God the Son and God the Holy Ghost because these expressions are our expressions.

The word 'Spirit' certainly is in our vocabulary, but we should not consider it to be a revelation, but a pointer to what is completely beyond the horizon for us and what will always be beyond us. Only our soul can be aware of Its Presence.

The spiritual values of our activities return to our souls

The acquisition by the soul of the spiritual values coming back from the person's activities is a fixed procedure and cannot be influenced by the person. However, the result of this procedure can still be modified. The person would certainly not want to change the positive, sanctifying values because their presence in his subconsciousness or in his awareness only enhances his state of being.

It is the negative values which, right from the beginning, do not harmonise with the Godly core of the soul and the positive values which have been acquired by this core – it is the negative values which, when they return to his subconsciousness or awareness, introduce their disquiet, unhappiness and tension. They cannot fail to bring with themselves the conflict and controversy which arise from their incompatibility with the Godly core of the soul.

The negative and destructive nature of sin activates itself at the moment the person becomes aware of it. As long as an activity which is wrong in the eyes of the Lord is merely a deposit on the outer area of the soul, sin is only a potentially negative force. When this negative value moves into the personality of its bearer and when he becomes aware of it, sin leaves its dormant state. To know what is right or wrong in the eyes of the Lord makes sin a reality within us. This knowledge virtually creates sin by converting it to a force which is able to join the other forces which operate within us.

It is said in the Scriptures that Christ took all our sins upon Himself and sacrificed Himself to cleanse us. This is the powerful manifestation of the Unconditional Love of our Heavenly Father. It is a constant offer to everyone to reverse the process of negative values attaching themselves to his soul and weighing it down. As our human nature cannot avoid producing negative values, this constant offer of forgiveness is the viable means of counteracting our human failings. Not through activities generating positive values can we hope to smother or outweigh the negative values. These negative values have to be removed, removed by the Grace and Mercy of our Heavenly Father on the basis of our faith in Him. This faith inspires our prayers and we pray that this faith may also express itself in the way we live.

God's Love for the world

> For God so loved the world that he gave his only Son, that whoever believes in him should not perish but have eternal life. (John 3:16).

God has loved the world – this means that He has loved His entire Creation, everything and everybody. He did not specify whom He loved or what He loved, He did not select, He included all. It was not even a question of including all because the word 'include' infers that a decision of this nature had been made.

There was no decision because a decision is the result of an assessment, of a judgement. A judgement in turn implies the possibilities of approval and disapproval, of acceptance and rejection. In our case, as we are dealing with God's relationship with us human beings, rejection means condemnation.

This statement about God's Unreserved Love did not apply only to the world as it was during Christ's lifetime, but it expressed the Lord's attitude also regarding the world prior to Christ. In Jeremiah 31:20 we read:

> Is Ephraim my dear son?
> Is he my darling child?
> For as often as I speak against him,
> I do remember him still.
> Therefore my heart yearns for him;
> I will surely have mercy on him,
>   says the LORD.

Even more significantly for us, these words point into the future, the entire future, till the end of the world. The Lord said that He would be with us till the end of this world. What about after that? After the end of THIS world there will be HIS Kingdom.

God's Love is unconditional, it was unconditional in the days of Christ, it was unconditional before Christ and, more importantly for us, it has been unconditional since the days of Christ. It has been so for all the generations born in the past and it will be so for all the generations yet to be born in the future. Unconditional for all yet to be born: the most wonderful promise. There is no alternative to this. The alternative, if there were one, would be that some of those yet to be born would – before they even see the light of this world – be condemned already. Condemned for what? Not for their transgressions. They have not yet done anything wrong, they have not even done anything yet. If there is no unconditional love for a human being before he is born, there must be judgment for this unborn human being.

Judgment of the unborn human being must then also be arbitrary. Judgment must result in the arbitrary condemnation of some of the unborn human beings. Our Lord is a Loving God. There is only one possibility: the Lord reaches out to every unborn, filling him and surrounding him with His Unconditional Love.

Does the flow of unconditional love stop abruptly when the human being opens his eyes and starts to breathe, begins his life here on earth? Certainly not. Now that the newborn baby is part of this world, he is just as much filled and surrounded by this Divine Love, by a love which is so wonderful, so boundless, so precious, so much beyond our understanding. This love is personified by God's only begotten Son Jesus Christ, by His person and by His sacrifice. We revere Him as our Saviour.

. . . that whoever believes in him should not perish but have eternal life.

The assurance that we will not perish if we believe in Christ also takes in our faith in God the Father and God the Holy Ghost. We cannot believe in just one part of the Holy Trinity, we either believe in the entire Holy Trinity or we do not believe.

The assurance that we will not perish if we believe refers to our life here on earth because to perish is a process restricted to our earthly situation. There is no perishing, no destruction, no ceasing to exist, no death in the hereafter, there is only eternal life. What survives the earthly existence is indestructible, ever-lasting, eternal, has not had a beginning and will not have an end. What survives the earthly existence is, by necessity, divine. What survives our worldly existence is our soul, our portion of God, the God in us.

Christ Himself, in John 10:34, refers to Psalm 82:6 which reads:

> I say, 'You are gods,
>   sons of the Most High, all of you;
> nevertheless, you shall die like men,
>   and fall like any prince.'

55

Soul, Spirit, Ghost

For the believer whose usual concern does not go beyond his personal requirements of his faith, some expressions used in the Bible and especially some of the terminology used by the theologians can create difficulties for his understanding and, therefore, a certain amount of uncertainty in his belief. The words 'soul, spirit, ghost', when used in close proximity, can fall into this category.

Let us look first at the word 'ghost' in its theological meaning. We read: 'a spirit; the soul of man; a spirit appearing after death, an apparition'.(1) Another dictionary lists: 'spirit, principle of life, life itself; soul'.(2) Our present word 'ghost' comes from Old English 'gást' and both are related to the present-day German word 'Geist'.(3)

The entry in the etymological dictionary for 'spirit' in its theological meaning gives the following: 'vital principle; the soul; a disembodied soul; a ghost'. We also read: 'spiritualisation; spiritualism, a being spiritual; the philosophical doctrine that nothing is real but soul or spirit; the doctrine that spirit has a real existence apart from matter'. The origin of the word is given as 'Latin "spiritus", a breath; "spirare", to breathe'.(4)

This information about the origin of the words 'spirit' and 'ghost' shows that although they are of different origin, their theological meanings are identical. Therefore, the grouping 'soul, spirit, ghost' reduces itself to 'soul, spirit'. Theological meanings of the word 'soul' are given as 'a spirit, embodied or disembodied; innermost being or nature'. This word comes from the Old English 'sáwol' which is related to the present-day German word 'Seele'.(5)

It is important to consult one more dictionary to consider the words 'soul, spirit' from another angle.

Some of the entries referring to the word 'soul' and relevant to our purpose are: 'theologically the immortal substance of man which distinguishes him from the beasts: "the immortality of the soul". A departed, disembodied spirit: "the souls of the blessed in heaven" '.(6)

For the word 'spirit' we find amongst others the following entries; 'breath; breeze; breath of life; life; soul; (translating Greek "pneuma", or Latin "spiritus" and "anima"): "the spirit shall return to God who gave it" '. Furthermore we read: 'this element or principle thought of as separated from the body; disembodied intelligence: "the spirits and souls of the righteous" '. We also find 'contrasted with matter: "God is pure

56

spirit." '(7)

The word 'soul' is used as a synonym for 'spirit'. Equally, the word 'spirit' is used as a synonym for the word 'soul'. This clearly establishes the fact that in essence 'soul' and 'spirit' have the same meaning in a theological context. To use a more everyday turn of phrase, soul and spirit are the same thing. Although they are identical in meaning, these two words are not freely interchangeable in their use.

This coupling of the equivalents of 'soul' and 'spirit' also exists in some other languages, for instance in German (Seele, Geist), French (âme, esprit) and Spanish (alma, espiritu).

To use the words 'soul' and 'spirit' side by side is actually saying things twice. This kind of usage is quite a common phenomenon in languages and is known as 'pleonasm'. However, here we are not dealing merely with a linguistic aspect. It could well be that the situation is also a reflection of the difficulties which exist for man before God: the eternal struggle to grasp the Divine and to express It in words. These two words may be considered a double effort in this undertaking.

Since they are possibly not normally used in conjunction, these two words have assumed separate identities. This has also been facilitated by the fact that their meanings are very abstract, that their meanings are very elusive because they lie far beyond the bounds of complete human understanding. It is not surprising, therefore, that these separate identities have, in the understanding of some people, led to the notion that 'soul' and 'spirit' have separate meanings.

The development of two separate meanings for two synonyms is well within normal language usage, as it is in the nature of a living language to change constantly. This constant change is based on the interaction between the language and the language user. Because we think in words, because our thoughts present themselves in expressions and sentences, there is a simultaneous interaction. Using an established language form, our thinking is, to some extent, shaped by our language. Finding our language form, to some extent, restrictive, our thinking modifies the language to suit its needs better.

To return to the separate identities of 'soul' and 'spirit' which may have led to different meanings in some people's minds, we must consider far-reaching consequences. Since these two words with two different meanings are the starting points of thoughts and deliberations and from then on offer themselves as tools for the same process, they may have given a new direction – their direction, in fact – to some believers' faith and doctrine formulating this faith.

If soul and spirit were considered to be two separate substances and the human being were considered to possess both, then they would have to be different. One would have to be different from the other. That this is not so, that we were granted one portion of our Lord – which we call either soul or spirit – is shown by these two quotations from the Bible:

> The Lord is my shepherd, . . . he restores my soul. (Psalm 23:1-3).
>
> Then Jesus, crying with a loud voice, said, 'Father, into thy hands I commit my spirit!' (Luke 23:46).

(1) *Chambers Etymological Dictionary*
(2) *The Universal Dictionary of the English Language*
(3) *Chambers Etymological Dictionary*
(4) ibid.
(5) ibid.
(6) *The Universal Dictionary of the English Language*
(7) ibid.

Further comment regarding the word 'Spirit'

In *The Universal English Dictionary*(1) we also find the following entry under 'spirit': '(2a) The immortal, non-material part of, or element in, man, which wills, thinks, and feels.'

'The immortal, non-material' part of man referred to in this instance is obviously man's portion of the Holy Ghost, his soul. We are told that this divine part of his person carries out surprisingly human functions: it 'wills, thinks and feels'. The explanation for this is quite straightforward: the Love of the Lord and His Will are in man's soul, and, in this soul, they transform themselves into activities and values which are part of the living process of man.

In addition to this, however, there is the willing, thinking and feeling which does not arise from the immortal, non-material part of man – but from his transient, physical part. As a result, the motivation is purely human, having been generated by the human part of man: his mind and his body. In the Bible this human part of man is often referred to as the 'flesh'.

The combination of divine and human parts within man results in an energy field between these two, with energy surges flowing back and forth. Or one element may completely dominate the other, or again there may be no noticeable energy field at all.

In the glossary of *The Bible according to Martin Luther's Translation,* we find further details about the situation within the human being. Under the heading 'Flesh' (German *Fleisch*) in the figurative sense we find the relevant information in paragraph 2 which translates as follows:

> However, the notion of 'flesh' is qualified in the negative sense: when Paul uses it to describe how the thinking, the exercising of his will and the acting of man is not determined by God and His Will, but only by the elements of this world, by human, all-too-human elements, even by sin (Romans 8:1-17; Galatians 5:13-6:2; Ephesians 2:3; Philippians 3:3,4). In contrast with the words 'Holy Ghost', the word 'flesh' describes the fact that sin has assumed such power over man and his body, that his 'flesh', like a foreign power, determines his whole being and leads him into death. (Romans 7:5-25). In contrast to this situation there is the 'Holy Ghost' through which God in the person of Christ takes hold of man, saves him and motivates him to act in love and self-discipline, leading him to eternal life.

It is important that some comments are added to the above quotation.

We read about man without being told that God dwells within him as his soul. Therefore we miss out on the vital information that man's conflict with God takes place within him: between his divine soul and his physical mind/body.

Because man's soul and its divine quality are not mentioned, the nature of sin cannot be presented clearly: sin is the outcome of the disobedience of the mind/body to the counselling put forward by the soul. This makes sin a product of the mind/body. Sin is not an original part of man like soul, mind and body. Therefore it is not sin which leads man into disaster, but it is mind and body when they forge their own destiny together by themselves.

(1) *The Universal Dictionary of the English Language.*

In defence of . . .

No church has the moral right to lecture or to judge a religious breakaway group. Once a church has been established as an organisation

59

for a certain time, some of its members may find it necessary to found their own variation of the mother church. This seems to be a continuous and thoroughly natural process. It should be borne in mind that throughout the history of the Christian church breakaway groups were sometimes derided, attacked, even cursed and persecuted. And yet, some who survived are now recognised and accepted as established churches.

The rivalry and competition among the various Christian churches, in this case as to who preaches and represents the Word of God more accurately, is nothing new. Indeed, it calls to mind an episode among the disciples: they made comparisons among themselves. Luke (22:24) puts it this way: 'A dispute also arose among them, which of them was to be regarded as the greatest.' In Mark (9:35) we read Christ's reaction: 'And he sat down and called the twelve; and he said to them, "If any one would be first, he must be last of all and servant of all." '

If there is more than one church which says that it is a Bible-believing church, then questions will appear. Churches which claim to be Bible-believing have some explaining to do as to why and how they are different from each other. If they differ considerably in doctrine, then a wit might ask whether each of these Bible-believing churches has its own individual Bible. The variety of denominations or churches encourages the question: 'Is there such an institution which can claim to preach the only correct Christian faith?' If there is such a church, then none of the other churches which are different can be considered to represent the correct doctrine.

If denominations which differ substantially from each other sincerely maintain that they preach the true Christian doctrine, then another question makes itself heard. People will ask: 'Is there such a thing as the one and only true Christian doctrine?' Quite obviously one is led to believe that there cannot be one Christian doctrine beside which there is no other valid Christian doctrine.

Somebody searching for the simple truth in that area – and the truth is always simple – concludes that he has to search in a different direction. The fact that there is one God is the pinnacle of the Christian faith. It is supported by varying Christian belief systems like the sharp point of a pyramid is supported by the massive body of the rest of the structure.

The varying Christian belief systems combine, like the main body of the pyramid, to strive upwards towards their climax, the supreme tenet of the Christian faith: 'There is one God.' There is no line of upward thrust in a pyramid which is identical with another line of upward thrust. Each one is different from the other. They all have to be different so that they all point to and move towards the pinnacle. They all have to be different so that they eventually meet in their highest point.

There have to be different religions and even variations within each one of them so that they can have one thing in common: the endeavour to move towards the Supreme Spirit which in the Christian religion we call 'God'. Each one of these belief systems, notwithstanding the frailty of human nature, is heading for the same goal. Whether the individual belief system chooses the shortest route, whether it travels on the smoothest road, whether it becomes bogged down in its self-inflicted difficulties, whether for some time it has little sense of direction, whether it is being overshadowed and almost put out of existence by another belief system – all these various aspects pale into insignificance before the word 'faith'.

The essence of each denomination, of each church, is not its doctrine, not its organisation, it is its individual members. And the most important attribute of each member of a religious body is his faith. In this sense the word 'faith' means 'relationship with God'. This relationship with God is the most direct, most independent, most unassailable line of communication there ever was or there ever will be. It is the lifeline between a person's soul and his Lord and Creator. The sublime, spiritual nature of God and our souls lifts this relationship out of the physical context of any religious organisation and puts it on a plane where there is nothing but God and the souls of His children.

It is a great comfort to know that these circumstances are a wonderful safeguard for the believer. He cannot be in the 'wrong' church the membership of which would 'disqualify' him from God's Unconditional Love. His direct line of communication with God cannot be interfered with if he clings to it. If his prayers come from his soul, his prayers will be heard, no matter what words or ritual he uses. When he prays earnestly, it is of no consequence what day of the week it is or what time of day it is. If he prays in a church, it does not matter what this church looks like from the outside or from the inside. What matters is his religious experience, the wonderful experience the human being has in the Presence of his God.

You have been saved

For by grace you have been saved through faith; and this is not your own doing, it is the gift of God – not because of works, lest any man should boast. (Ephesians 2:8,9).

What if somebody cannot believe? Is the ability to believe a gift from God which He bestows upon the soul, or is belief the result of the person's decision, the result of an effort, the response to an outside influence?

If belief is a gift from the Lord which He bestows upon the soul then faith is a sign of His Grace and Favour which He grants to a human being. Instead of: 'You will be saved by your faith and the grace of the Lord' the non-believer can be told: 'Since you have not received the gift of faith from the Lord in this lifetime, you will be saved by the Grace of the Lord alone.'

If the belief is the result of a person's decision, the result of an effort or the response to an outside influence, then it appears that the believer himself made a contribution to receive his faith. Is this contribution equivalent to being one of his works as in 'nobody will be saved through his own works'? No, it is not, simply because the person did not and could not produce his faith nor could he acquire this faith somewhere. Faith is not a state of body, it is not a state of mind. It is a state of soul, it is the awareness of the soul of its divine nature. What happened when a person became a believer was not a flow of action from his mind/body part to his soul, but in the opposite direction. His soul counselled his mind/body part, created favourable conditions in it and provided the stimulus for a decision, for an effort, or the response to an outside influence. Quite clearly, the starting point of his move towards faith lay in his soul 'for God is at work in you, both to will and to work for his good pleasure'. (Philippians 2:13). There is even more specific reference to our point under discussion in the following Bible passages:

No one can come to me unless the Father who sent me draws him; (John 6:44).
This is why I told you that no one can come to me unless it is granted him by the Father. (John 6:65).
. . . and no one can say 'Jesus is Lord' except by the Holy Spirit. (1 Corinthians 12:3).

The Lord always takes the initiative, whether it is obvious or not. The Lord made the soul communicate its awareness to the mind/body part of the person. To put it concisely: The Lord, in the person's soul kindled the desire for faith and the person made this divine desire his own decision. Faith is a gift from God. Even the desire to believe is a gift from God. There is no other faith beside that.

The new self

The inquiring mind points its activities in a certain direction which, to some extent at least, can be determined by the nature of this mind. This fact sets the boundaries of the mind's activities either relatively close together or spaces them relatively far apart.

Not only are we dealing with the scope of these activities, but we also have to be aware of their method. We must remember that our thinking as a collective experience found itself originally face to face with our tangible environment which was perceived mainly through our five senses. Of course, the so-called sixth sense would immediately have played a part. Thus directed at tangible targets and then reflected back to us from them, our thinking assumed a certain finality. In the course of daily existence, successive situations occurred which had to be dealt with by the mind. A conclusion or an end was needed before the next situation could come under consideration. This method was required not only by the nature of our surroundings, but also by the fundamental role our thinking played in the process of our survival. This thinking obviously helped to maintain our physical existence, but it also was and still is a key factor in the survival of our inner being.

While early man, in his daily routine, found himself carried along by the broad flow of what was happening around him, he soon realised his potential to alter his surroundings to suit his needs better. This marked the beginning of a process of separation: man set himself apart from the world around him. And this process became stronger and stronger, not only growing in intensity, but also broadening its scope. In fact, man – consciously or subconsciously – plays the part of someone who 'has dominion over the world'. Whether he has acquired the necessary knowledge and understanding of this world around him and whether he acknowledges and respects the fact that he himself and whatever is around him initially was and since then has been the work of our Creator – these considerations must be put aside for the moment.

Man feels that he occupies a position of power. His survival instinct as well as his conscious efforts to satisfy his ambitions effectively give this power his highest priority. This power lies in his thinking and his language. In his mind man creates an image of the world around him in part through perceptions and the resulting process of questions and answers which are all determined by his ability. One could even say that he creates his image of the world through his questions. As a result, the answers are somewhat predetermined by the limitations of the questions. In the end a precarious situation may arise if this limited image of the world combines with the survival instinct and ambitions. The result is this: man faces the possibility that in his mind he decides what is and what is not.

When the mind deals with tangible situations, the finding of what is and what is not can be adjusted relatively easily.

However, when the mind is focused on abstract notions, the adjustment is far more complex. There are basic requirements, such as: the silencing of the survival instinct, the abandonment of any desire for power and the investigation of one's method of thinking. In other words: a complete surrender of one's identity. What appears to be at first glance total self-destruction is actually the moment of complete rebirth, the birth of the new self.

The new self will be growing into a very different person, into a very spiritual person. Not only will the person be different, but the world will be a different world as perceived by the person. What he had been familiar with previously will appear in a new light. Entirely new areas of a spiritual nature will open up to him. The process will not be so much an acquisition of understanding, that is, an activity of the mind in the first place.

It will be growth in the form of an increasing awareness which is an activity of the soul. From this will then spring a new kind of understanding which, being spiritual in nature, will combine with the spiritual awareness of the soul. The soul will be filled to capacity by this combination and the capacity of the soul will constantly grow. Some people will prefer to use the word 'faith' instead of 'spiritual awareness and spiritual understanding'. Some may even give this combination a name which they have found themselves.

However, let us always remember that for the new self the importance and validity of his previous, traditional perception has ceased to exist. Now that he is moving along with the flow, being carried as if embedded in its general thrust, his perceptions and subsequent decisions are in tune with the spirit of this new direction. And the dimension of the new self is this: what he cannot perceive because of his human limitations, what perhaps he does not even endeavour to perceive, does exist for him nevertheless. It exists for him as an area of awareness, of understanding and of acceptance.

This development, this spiritual growth, will permeate the whole person. The spiritual content of his life will increase to such a level that when his life here on earth draws to a close, when the body falls away from the soul, it will only be a stage along a natural progression, it will not be an end. It will not be death, but the beginning of a new life. For the soul it will be like going through a passage with a wonderfully bright light at the opening ahead. This experience has been confirmed by many people who have had near-death experiences. Our transition will be as simple as stepping through a door.

The Kingdom of God is happening

It has been said that great changes are under way: Jesus Christ is coming back into this world; that is, He is coming back into our hearts.

This is a very appropriate way of expressing a spiritual happening, of clothing it in words of our usual language patterns.

Another way of describing the same situation could start with the concept that Jesus has always been in our hearts, Jesus and His Father and the Holy Ghost. God has always been in us; our soul is our portion of God. What is happening now is a more obvious, a more accelerated process of us becoming aware of the Lord's Presence in us, of the divine nature of our soul.

Our spiritual journey is gathering pace. Yet, we are not going anywhere, neither in the physical way, nor are we moving into different spiritual areas. This spiritual journey is taking place within us. As our concept of time and place is of no consequence to the Spirit, our spiritual journey can and in fact does take place within us. We are moving towards the Father who said of Himself that He is the Truth. We are moving towards Him, towards the Truth, at the same rate as we are becoming aware of His Divine Presence within us. This increasing awareness also allows us to become more and more aware of His Presence around us. His Presence also appears as His Will which is constantly at work, constantly creating, constantly changing. His Will creates change. Great is the Will of the Lord. Great are the changes under way within us and around us.

Heavenly bodies

The idea that heavenly bodies have direct and varying influence on us, for instance our behaviour, emotional state and bodily functions, is accepted by some and rejected by others.

Ancient people had wide knowledge of the close connection between the positions and trajectories of the heavenly bodies and natural phenomena on earth, the heavenly body we live on. No wonder that they worshipped some, elevating them to the rank of creators, of gods. Many of our contemporaries, to some degree, respond along similar lines. If they accept in their minds what mankind has known for some considerable time, they may be inclined to think also that the heavenly bodies create the influences which have been attributed to them. Although there is no harm in this attitude, it may not only be frowned on and refuted, but also branded as an aberration from a valid belief in God. As such it may be considered to be an association with some sort of cult, even with witchcraft.

There is absolutely no reason why the acknowledgment of the interaction between the heavenly bodies – including our planet earth and whatever is found on it – is not unreservedly compatible with a belief in God. We acknowledge God as 'the Creator of Heaven and of Earth'. He is the only creator, we know that. He created the universe according to His plan. Because the heavenly bodies are His Creation, they are an expression of His Will, a physical expression of His Will. As such they play their part in the overall scheme devised by our Lord. Let us not give credit to the servants for the missions which were assigned to them by their Master.

God is all and in all

We must imagine that the soul is not a hermetically closed unit, surrounded by a membrane. It is rather an energy which, as pure energy, is not associated with any physical aspect. It is not physical energy, but spiritual energy, it is not subject to any limitations such as time and place. Therefore this energy may divide and merge with other energies, it may absorb parts of other energies or even whole energies. In the entire energy field the possibilities of combinations are absolutely unlimited. Because of the constant and free combinations and variations, the whole spectrum of each energy may change continually.

This constant interplay of energies is, to some extent, like certain aspects of a planetary constellation: there is constant movement and each participant constantly influences the other participants in their direction and even their very substances while simultaneously being influenced by them.

In this spiritual world, if we may use this rather absurd term, there is absolute order or – much more appropriately put – there is absolute harmony. The reason is very simple and very profound: the Lord manifests Himself as His Will and His Will is His Energy. It is true that the Lord is Creator of all, but putting it like this is only a necessary concession to the limitations of our human understanding. In the spiritual world the Lord need not be called the Creator because He actually IS the Spiritual World. And this spiritual world is energy, entirely and completely His Energy. The Lord IS His Energy.

The words of a hymn come to mind: 'Oh God, from whom all blessings flow . . .' in the form of His Will which is His Energy, which is He Himself. It is true what has been said that there is 'one God and Father of us all, who is above all and through all and in all'. (Ephesians 4:4-6).

Nearer, my God, to Thee

The question of vibrations is of fundamental importance in our relationship with God. Not so much as it affects the Divine Nature of the Lord and His Attitude to us, His children, but as it affects our perception of our Heavenly Father.

Our awareness of the continuous Presence of the Lord is the perception of Him as He reveals Himself in our souls. This awareness communicates itself to the mind and the result is what we call 'faith'.

This combined perception of our Heavenly Father is commensurate with our ability to receive His Image within the range of the frequency of each individual's vibrations. To journey on the path of our spiritual development, in the above context, means that this continuous progress raises our vibrations. The vibrational rate of each individual is entirely his personal characteristic which puts him in the same grouping only with other individuals who have reached the same frequency, but puts him at variance with other groupings. He can no longer identify completely with the belief of individuals who have a lower frequency. He can not yet completely identify with the belief of individuals who have a higher frequency. However, in the latter circumstance he would derive great benefit for his own progress, be it an instantly increased awareness or an input which will set to work within him.

The preceding thoughts clearly show that faith, as well as its expression in thought and word, is a highly individual matter. It is the result of a highly individual development. Any belief system which attempts to govern this individual development holds the individual at a certain point and, through its doctrine which demands adherence to a uniform standard, prevents this individual from progressing along the path of his spiritual journey.

In the Old Testament (2 Moses 19:12,13,21-24) it is stated that the human being of those days could not survive to see the Lord face to face. The human being of our days would suffer the same fate. To the people of the Old Testament the Lord was a person. To the people of our days there is the Holy Trinity, consisting of God the Father, God the Son and God the Holy Ghost. Whether this concept is accepted by all Christians is not the point here. For those who accept it, it has loosened up the concept of God as a person, made it more abstract or, to use a more appropriate way of putting it: the concept of the Holy Trinity has moved God further away from the physical and into the centre of the spiritual. This has paved the way for the realisation that God has revealed Himself to us as His Divine Will, His Divine Energy which pervades His entire Creation. As the concept of the Holy Trinity took some time to establish itself – Athanasius (295-373) was one of its protagonists – the concept of God being for us His Will, His Divine Energy, will gradually find more general acceptance.

Those of us who, through the Grace of God, have travelled sufficiently far along the road of their spiritual development happily acknowledge that the Lord's Divine Energy is, in fact, THE Spiritual Energy of the whole universe. This spiritual energy is of such a high vibrational frequency that it is entirely beyond our comprehension and tolerance. Any human being, no matter how advanced in his spiritual growth, would be instantly consumed when encountering it.

This immeasurable difference in vibrations was overcome by our Heavenly Father by sending His Son Jesus Christ into our world. Jesus was a combination of inconceivable Divine Energy and the very low human vibrational frequency. He constantly transformed His Holiness into a vibrational frequency which our human nature could cope with. In other words, He brought God the Father down to our level of perception, understanding and metaphysical capacity.

Being the son of man and the Son of God in itself is the essence of His mission. This revolutionised our relationship with God and overturned some of the religious dogma of the Old Testament and all of the authority of the clergy of the days of the Old Testament. That is why they crucified Him.

What the Lord did for the whole of mankind in one big undertaking by sending His Son into our world – this He has been doing also for the individual person one by one. He has been lowering his vibrational frequency far enough for each individual so that He is to him like a beacon for a ship: to guide, encourage, protect and bless this individual, to help him along – closer to His Holiness. Already during our life here on earth we can say with the writer of one of our many hymns: 'nearer, my God, to thee'. It is both a motto pointing into the future and a joyful acknowledgment of an accomplished fact.

Apparitions coming to us from the hereafter

It appears that when the soul leaves the body it takes with it characteristics of the earthly person's personality. We get this impression because when such a soul returns and visits us we may perceive this apparition in the same physical form as we had known the person during his life here on earth. Not only may we see the person as we remember him, but this person may also act and react as we remember him. This encounter may take place during a meditation, in a state of trance or bordering on a trance, or even during complete awareness. In other words, this apparition may appear before our inner eye or right in front of our own eyes. We may have the impression that the person appears within us or right in front of us.

This phenomenon does not happen only between two beings who had known each other before, but it may also take place between total strangers. And yet, the apparition has the personal qualities which the person had while he was here on earth as subsequent checks will confirm. Such an encounter may also bring to light experiences this person had had here on earth which are proved true when inquiries are made.

This makes us wonder whether the soul takes with it some or all of the personal characteristics which the person had here on earth. However, this is not so, it may only seem so. In order to be perceived by us within our own range of perception, the soul has to assume such qualities as are part of our own experience. It has to manifest itself to us in a way which is meaningful.

When the Lord makes an approach

When the Lord makes an approach to us human beings He initiates a relationship with us. Whether we regard this as something which applies to a specific incident, a particular situation or whether we consider it to be a constant and endless relationship – that is of little concern. The important fact is that the Lord does seek us every moment of our lives. He is with us – within us – all the time, always. That means that His Goodness, His Kindness, His Grace and His Favour are consistently flowing to us. This is the Lord's part of our relationship with Him.

And what is our part? Do we have to do anything specific to initiate the manifestation of the Lord's Love for us, or to assure its continuous out-pouring to us? The answer is very simple and consists of a very humble 'no'. We do not have to do anything. And if we make an effort to do something to show our readiness to accept Him, if we go some way in His direction to welcome His Love, that will certainly please Him. However, our positive reaction is not the motivation for the Lord to treat us as His children. Our negative reaction or a total absence of a reaction on our part is not a deterrent either for the Lord to treat us as His children. The Lord manifests His Divine Nature irrespective of what else or who else may exist beside Him. He does not show goodness, kindness, grace, favour and unconditional love as a person would do it. He is His Goodness, He is His Kindness, He is His Grace, He is His Favour and He is His Unconditional Love. These are some of the innumerable ways the Divine Energy may manifest itself.

We must never be so presumptuous as to think or say that our attitude, actions or reactions have any bearing on the Lord's attitude to us. Yet, it has been maintained that, if man does something which is pleasing in the eyes of the Lord, then the Lord will love him. Equally, if man does something which is an abomination to the Lord, then the Lord will direct His wrath to him. This is the spirit of the Old Testament. This, to some extent, is also the spirit of part of the New Testament. To put it differently, the human being has effectively been credited with the ability to exercise an influence over the Lord, to influence His Behaviour, not only towards man as an individual but also towards mankind collectively. The various kinds of offerings come to mind, such as cereal offerings and burnt offerings, which were an important part of the ritual of the days of the Old Testament. Their purpose was to express gratitude and to win the favour of the Lord. This type of sacrifice was also offered by the adherents of pre-God cults to express gratitude and to win the favour of their gods. Same motivation, same action, only a different destination. The Jews of the Old Testament, obviously, could lay claim to be well above the followers of pre-God cults because they were bringing sacrificial offerings to the one and only God. The Lord, however, quite clearly indicated that He despised these offerings saying that, instead of bringing vain offerings, His children should mend their ways. (Isaiah 1:10-17). However, one thing is sure, the Lord always hears our prayers, He always listens to us and He always responds in His own time and in His Own Way.

How was it possible for the concept to come about that our actions would win us favour with God? How could this idea be cultivated and believed? Does God love us because 'we do the right thing'? One of the main reasons has been that the Lord has been personified. This did not happen by design, but out of sheer necessity. The first step in dealing with the unknown, the new, is to master it with some known, well-established formula of thought and language, or a modification of such a formula.

For the ancient people spirits were therefore given masculine or feminine gender. The Lord Himself concurred with this practice and revealed Himself as our Heavenly Father, for example. It is also significant that the Lord assumed a male identity, the more prestigious and more suitable gender out of male and female. As a result, God has been a male personification right throughout the Bible. In general, human thinking cannot burst through the boundaries and barriers of language because it uses language forms from the very moment of inspiration. Many people have now reached an awareness of the Divine beyond the level of the average believer because they by-passed the concept of God being a person, being a God in the image of man. It is quite possible that this same awareness cannot be shared easily by others because of the constraints imposed by the existing terminology. The words 'God, Lord, Heavenly Father, Creator' and others are sufficiently spiritual in themselves to set Him clearly apart from man. However, the words ' he, him, his' introduce the human aspect where it is not needed, not desired and where it can be quite detrimental. The solution? An entirely new and unique set of pronouns. New words are constantly created, but generally under more favourable circumstances, one must admit.

It is completely unimportant how God has been presented, whether with a flowing beard or not, whether sitting on a throne pronouncing judgment, or in the person of His Son Jesus Christ standing in the middle of His disciples. In the Bible words are used to present God as a person and in various art forms we have met God presented as a person.

The essential characteristic of a person is that his feelings, his thoughts and his actions are produced by him. There is a dual aspect: the person himself and whatever emanates from him. Let us consider the person first. He may be happy, angry, kind, unforgiving – just to mention a few qualities. Whatever comes from this person may be a true reflection of his nature. On the other hand, it may be quite different from his true inner being. For instance, a very peaceful person may be provoked to do what is not at all in keeping with his character.

The personification of God for reasons of language and thinking has allowed us to accommodate Him in our spiritual and intellectual world. We had to make Him as human as possible so that we can understand Him – accepting at the same time that His Thoughts are not our thoughts and His Ways are not our ways. We have not only been thinking with our minds, but we have also been believing with our minds. These statements are not critical or judgemental, they are simply an observation about a stage of the development of our belief system. The world of the Old Testament was such a stage which was followed by a tremendous development, the New Testament – note the word 'New'. This New Testament or new covenant, heralded a break-through on our path towards God's Kingdom on Earth. By the Grace of God we are moving in the direction of His Kingdom on Earth by moving in His direction. The Kingdom of God is within, so it has been said and written. (Luke 17:20,21). The advent of His Kingdom on Earth is therefore also being prepared within us, in our innermost being. One of the aspects of this preparation within us is an increasing awareness of the divine nature of our soul, an increasing awareness of the Kingdom of God within us. This appears also as an increasing attunement of us to the Divine within us and around us. It may also be called an increasing understanding with our hearts, that is with our souls, not with our minds because God lies beyond our minds but God is in our souls.

Consideration must be given to the works done by the believer. It has been said that faith without works is dead. This is quite correct, but it must be works which do not have an ulterior motive. If they were calculated to be noted by the Lord in some kind of record in favour of the individual's salvation, they would be futile. The reason being that man will not be saved through his works, but through his faith and the Grace of God – in actual fact just by the Grace of God alone. God grants the gift of faith and, by doing so, creates a believer. This gift of faith fills the whole person. In turn it inspires the believer to transform the blessings he has received into actions which benefit his fellow-man. They are indeed works which are pleasing in the eyes of God, but they are inspired by God and not motivated by a human element.

This is the active part which man plays in his relationship with God: his faith and the manifestation of his faith in his way of life – both inspired by God. We are what we are by the Grace of God and we are able to do what we do also by the Grace of God.

The expulsion from Paradise

When Adam and Eve had been driven out of Paradise they were the first in a long line of generations who experienced our kind of human existence. That was the punishment of Adam and Eve for disobeying the Word of the Lord. Their punishment has been passed on from generation to generation and, yet, these subsequent generations have been totally unconnected with the original transgression. This line of thinking makes our Lord an utterly vengeful God.

When considering this matter, we should first try to clarify what Paradise is, or better, what we think it is. To us, one of the striking features of Paradise is the perfect peace and harmony, the complete balance. There is complete balance between the spiritual and the physical: plants, animals and Adam and Eve were all one. Even the physical is of spiritual nature in this complete oneness. And this is also the case in the hereafter. Therefore Paradise, where the human being took his beginning, and the hereafter where the human being returns in the end, are one and the same. Jesus Himself indicates this when, on the cross, He says to one of the robbers crucified with Him: 'Truly, I say to you, today you will be with me in Paradise.' (Luke 23:43).

If we believe that the Lord is the Creator of Heaven and Earth we must also believe that the snake which tempted Adam and Eve in Paradise was also part of this creation. Consequently the expulsion from Paradise was also part of the Lord's plan. Either we accept the Will of the Lord without reservation or we completely reject the notion that the Lord is totally in control. There is no doubt that the Lord is totally in control, whether it appears so to us or not.

Some people believe what is written in the Bible about Paradise, the temptation of Adam and Eve and their subsequent expulsion. They believe all this to be a factual account. Others believe it more like one believes the meaning of a parable, the parable of where man originally came from and how and why he is here on earth.

Obviously, one might say, the Lord had created Paradise and the earth. Paradise as the spiritual world where even bodies are of a spiritual nature, like angels. (Matthew 22:29,30; Luke 20:35,36). Earth as a predominantly physical world from the point of view of modern man. On earth we are surrounded by the spiritual and the physical. One might wonder whether the world, before the arrival of man, was generally a balanced and self-regulating unit of the universe, an earthly version of the Heavenly Paradise, so to speak.

Eating of the fruit of the forbidden tree opened the eyes of Adam and Eve and they realised that they were naked: they suddenly knew that they were also physical. This discovery is equivalent to our way of being born: at birth we become an individual combination of spiritual and physical elements. We may therefore understand the results of the temptation like this: firstly, Adam and Eve disobeyed the Lord's Word; secondly, having become aware of their physical bodies, they were then, in fact, physical and spiritual beings in a purely spiritual environment. Thirdly, the Lord was concerned that these two human beings would also eat fruit from the tree of life and live forever, as we read in Genesis chapter 3.

Of course, the Lord could have wiped the whole transgression of Adam and Eve if He had wanted to because He is the Almighty. Therefore we must conclude that the expulsion from Paradise happened because it was part of the Lord's plan. For the people of the Old Testament it made sense and for many people ever since it has made sense to accept the following: as descendants of Adam and Eve who were the first human beings and consequently the first sinners, we are in this world and not in Paradise because we are condemned to the same punishment as they were. This line of thinking makes our Lord an utterly vengeful God. Those who do not believe in this continuing punishment will refer to passages like Romans 8:15,16 where we read: '. . . you have received the spirit of sonship. When we cry, 'Abba! Father!' it is the Spirit himself bearing witness with our spirit that we are children of God . . .'

We have to say that our human existence is not punishment, but that human existence is simply what it is because it takes place in physical surroundings: our physical body is part of the physical world of this planet. At the same time our physical body is the home of a spiritual body, our soul. Thus our human existence – ranging from devastating lows to exhilarating highs – takes place in the energy field between these two poles: the spiritual and the physical. In fact, our human existence is this very energy field.

Reincarnation: merely a second-chance acquisition of life skills?

It has been found that, within the framework of reincarnation, souls come back into this world and – together with their newly-acquired minds and bodies – they attempt to improve on their performances in previous lifetimes.

It is quite true that skills, know-how, knowledge, experience – whatever we like to call it – acquired in a previous lifetime are remembered, are readily available when called upon in a subsequent lifetime. The word 'skills' implies that there is a line of activity going from the point of origin to a specific destination. This kind of activity cannot be a pure, self-contained and self-motivated activity because its nature is partly determined by its destination, its purpose.

In skills and knowledge there is a metaphysical content which can be isolated by a process of abstraction, of extraction, of distillation, so to speak. This may be likened to the extraction of essential oils from a plant. In our case, on the metaphysical level, the essence is extracted from each individual activity, each individual situation and from the total experience. And what are the properties of this essence?

This essence is a sublimation of all the essential qualities of skills and knowledge which had previously been used by the individual. This essence is so complex that it contains the potential response to any situation in which the skills and the knowledge in question are required. This essence is completely abstract, totally amorphous: we may say that it is a potential. We may also call it wisdom. And we may definitely call it energy. We may even say that it is a minute particle of the all-embracing truth.

Because of its metaphysical nature, the wisdom-energy is very compatible with the soul. It will bond with the soul and, as a storage facility for future lives, it will share the soul's permanency and indestructibility. When the soul is reincarnated the wisdom-energy will reconstitute itself and materialise, as required, to assume the nature of skills, know-how, knowledge and experience once more.

What has been said so far does not cover completely the mission of a reincarnated soul in a new lifetime. First, however, one must bear in mind that the reincarnation of a soul is never an act of punishment inflicted on this 'God within us'. The next thought must be directed to the assertion that in a new lifetime the new person is given the opportunity and, to some extent, the ability to do better this time round. By this we mean that the same opportunity as in a past life is provided again. The person in his totality of soul, mind and body is then induced by the circumstances or by his own decision alone to attempt a better response to the whole situation compared with a previous lifetime. This is generally regarded as a learning experience, as a process of acquiring certain skills, as a way of growing and developing.

The expression 'acquiring certain skills' refers to experiences on the physical level, including the mental and emotional aspects. The term 'growing and developing' refers to the benefits coming from these physical, mental and emotional experiences. In other words, there is firstly an enrichment on the physical, mental and emotional level and then a resulting enrichment on a higher plane which we may call the spiritual level.

Each and every activity of the human being has a spiritual ingredient which is embodied in the activity in the same way as our soul is contained in our body. And here again we enter the domain of vibrations. The positive nature of an activity raises the vibration of its spiritual element. Again, the positive activity on a physical, mental and emotional level enhances the situation on the spiritual level. This is the way to enjoy the blessings of God's Kingdom, His Kingdom which is in each one of us. And each of us is a labourer in God's vineyard, in His Kingdom.

The progression from a physical level to a spiritual level is neither surprising nor illogical because matter is vibration at a certain level or frequency. Furthermore, thoughts and feelings are vibrations because they are energies which vibrate at certain levels or frequencies. All is vibration.

We must not allow ourselves to be tied to the hereditary approach of thinking in terms of categories. This fragments not only the world around us but also the world within us. We must open ourselves up, we must hold out our hands to receive humbly and gratefully. We must cease to make our minds the measure of the Lord's Creation. We must not form a picture of the Lord's Creation in our minds first and then look at His Works, only to see them as we had already imagined them to be. We will find the answers to all our questions . . . No, the answers will come to us! Quite often the answers will come to us before we can even think of the questions! And one of these answers, one of these gifts is the realisation that there is a common denominator whose name is 'vibrations'.

In this light, the second-chance acquisition of skills by a person with a reincarnated soul takes on a new dimension. When we look deeper, we realise that it is actually a second-chance acquisition of higher vibrations. The skills are only a ways and means of raising the vibrations of the soul. At the same time, raising the vibrations of the soul also means raising the awareness of the soul of its divine nature. And this in turn means further progress on the journey towards God, a journey which takes place in our souls.

Where is there room for unconditional love?

For God so loved the world that he gave his only Son, that whoever believes in him should not perish but have eternal life. (John 3:16).

Our Heavenly Father sent His Son Jesus Christ into this world because He loves us. According to this passage His Love does not quite reach us, it stops short of us. According to this passage, we, each individual, have to bring this Divine Love to fruition. We have to make it effective by our contribution which is our faith in Christ. This Divine Love as expressed here is, in actual fact, aimed specifically at the believer, making eternal life possible for him, even assuring him of eternal life.

The unbeliever, no doubt, is part of the world also, part of the world which our Heavenly Father loves. Therefore he must also be loved by Him. However, he disqualifies himself from the ultimate benefit of the Lord's Love because he does not believe in Christ. He has no faith, he does not share the Christian faith. In other words, he has not yet received the gracious gift of faith from our Heavenly Father. In John 6:44 we read the words of Christ: 'No one can come to me unless the Father who sent me draws him.' That really means that the unbeliever does not disqualify himself, he simply is not included.

Since God's Love – in order to be love in real terms – is Unconditional Love which reaches out to everyone, the passage quoted from the Bible should be different. The letter of the text must be different to express the spirit of the text. Because the spirit of the text is unconditional love, the text should be as follows:

> For God so loved the world that he gave his only Son, that no one should perish but all have eternal life.

In the writing of the Apostle Paul we read:

> . . . you have received the spirit of sonship. When we cry, 'Abba! Father!' it is the Spirit himself bearing witness with our spirit that we are children of God and, if children, then heirs, heirs of God and fellow heirs with Christ, provided we suffer with him in order that we may also be glorified with him. (Romans 8:15-17).

This passage prompts the thought that, if we are children of God and were born sinners, then God created us sinners. In fact, the term 'sinner' does not allow us to see the situation as it is. God created us as we are: human beings with a soul, a mind and a body. The physical mind/body part of each of us causes us to be unable to live up to the guidelines placed in front of us: the Word of the Lord. The Lord knows all about that, He created us. He created us as we are, but, at the same time, He gave us the opportunity to cancel out our innate disabilities by granting us forgiveness of sins. This forgiveness of sins runs parallel, in time and place, with the committing of sins: sinning and forgiveness are simultaneous. It is within our souls that the awareness of sin can immediately be dissolved by the awareness of forgiveness.

Christ, visibly to all, expiated our sins. God the Father had already promised us His Love and His Forgiveness and His Word became flesh in His Son Jesus. Why should we suffer with Him? That would rob Christ's sacrifice of all its meaning, it would make it completely null and void, it would go against the Lord's Will.

Why do we have to suffer in order to be glorified, why do we have to do anything – apart from listening to the God within us and doing what we can to follow His Counsel? We are already glorified. What higher glory can a human being imagine than to be a child of God?

As to the glorification of Christ, His suffering for our sins has added glory to His name in our eyes. However, His real glorification is that of the Son of God, even before He came into this world, even before He came to be – because as part of God the Father and the Holy Ghost He is His Glorification, He has always been: His name is 'I am'. (John 8:58).

The spirit of the two passages quoted above is apparent in many parts of the Bible: the Lord is gracious unto us and immediately there follows a proviso, a condition. Sometimes it is not clear who imposes the condition, as in the first passage. Sometimes the condition is clearly from the writer, as in the second passage. To the reader, this combination of a gracious gift from God and an immediate condition attached to it can be quite bewildering. The condition destroys the nature of the gift and the situation is reminiscent of a transaction, a transaction of a quasi legal character.

This brings to mind the names of the two sections of the Bible, the Old Testament and the New Testament, meaning the two covenants of God. They are solemn and binding undertakings. They are promises made by God and demands made by God. They are agreements made by God with man. As a partner in these agreements, man has to play an active part, he has obligations, he has criteria to meet. This is more so in the Old Testament than in the New Testament. The New Testament – 'new' definitely meaning 'different' – was introduced by God with the mission of Christ because 'He so loved the world'. In Hebrews 8:6,7 we find the expression of the necessity for the New Testament from the human point of view: '. . . Christ has obtained a ministry which is as much more excellent than the old as the covenant he mediates is better, since it is enacted on better promises. For if that first covenant had been faultless, there would have been no occasion for a second.' Then the writer continues with verses 8-13: 'For he finds fault with them when he says: "The days will come, says the Lord, when I will establish a new covenant with the house of Israel and with the house of Judah; not like the covenant that I made with their fathers on the day when I took them by the hand to lead them out of the land of Egypt; for they did not continue in my covenant, and so I paid no heed to them, says the Lord. This is the covenant that I will make with the house of Israel after those days, says the Lord: I will put my laws into their minds, and write them on their hearts, and I will be their God, and they shall be my people. And they shall not teach every one his fellow or every one his brother, saying,

'Know the Lord,' for all shall know me, from the least of them to the greatest. For I will be merciful toward their iniquities, and I will remember their sins no more.' In speaking of a new covenant he treats the first as obsolete. And what is becoming obsolete and growing old is ready to vanish away.'

One of the main themes of the New Testament is God's Love for us, His children. However, the spirit of the Old Testament infiltrated parts of the New Testament, neutralising in those parts the manifestation of the new spirit of Divine Love. This state of affairs has been perpetuated by the use of the Old Testament in conjunction with the New Testament. This is generally not done to demonstrate the enormous difference, the wonderful, new grace and favour contained in the New Testament. The obsolete tenets of the Old Testament are generally given the same credibility and validity as 'The Good News for Modern Man'.(1)

The New Testament is obviously not only a statement of the various aspects of the Christian faith, but also a formulation of Christian doctrine to be put before the nations to guide them and help them as partners of agreements with God. In such a climate there is no room for unconditional love as the two passages quoted earlier show. There is instead judgement, reward and punishment. Even what we already are by the Grace of God, we are asked to strive for in order to be 'really' it. Consider the following:

> 'While you have the light, believe in the light, that you may become sons of light.' (John 12:36).

This should actually read: 'While you have the light, believe in the light, that you may remain sons of light.'

When we wonder and ask where there is room for unconditional love, we receive a rather unexpected answer: in the soul of each one of us, in 'the Kingdom within'. Our soul tells us that God is Unconditional Love. What our soul tells us we believe because when our soul speaks it is God who speaks since our soul is our portion of God. (Psalm 73:26). God's Love is Unconditional Love. Are there instances of unconditional love in the Bible which readily come to mind? Yes, already in 3 Moses 19:18 we read the commandment: '. . . you shall love your neighbour as yourself.' It is also written in Galatians 5:14 '. . . the whole law is fulfilled in one word, 'You shall love your neighbour as yourself.' Christ said that he had not come into the world to abolish the law, but to fulfil it. And fulfil the law He did with His death for us on the cross. It is also said that no-one can show greater love than the person who lays down his life for someone else. Christ is the personification of this love which does not ask questions or set conditions.(2) Jesus Christ the Son, God the Father and the Holy Ghost are One. Divine Love is what we like to call unconditional love, even though we know that the very nature of love is that it is unconditional.

It is worth our while to have a brief look at some of the information about the Old Testament and the New Testament given in *The Bible Timeline* and *The Bible According to Martin Luther's Translation*. In the genealogies of Genesis 1-11 in the traditional Hebrew Bible we find information concerning the first 20 generations of biblical patriarchs, accounting for 1946 years before the birth of Abraham. This would place the creation of Adam in about 3941 B.C. Non-biblical chronologies based on archaeological finds, for instance, differ greatly from biblical chronologies.

The year of Abraham's birth is given as 1995 B.C., but, like all other dates, it can be only approximate and relative to other dates. According to the same chronology Moses was born in 1355 B.C. and received the Ten Commandments inscribed on stone tablets in 1275 B.C. The year of David's birth is listed as 1034 B.C.

From about 760 B.C. onwards there are prophets like Amos, Isaiah, Micah, Jeremiah, to mention only a few.

In 1015 B.C. the Israelites began developing the Hebrew alphabet based on the earlier Canaanite alphabet. Between about 1000 B.C. and 200 B.C. the various parts of the Old Testament were written. About 300-130 B.C. the Old Testament was translated from Hebrew into Greek. Towards the end of the first century A.D. Jewish scribes in Palestine decided on the exact composition of the Hebrew Bible.

The first Gospel as we know it was that of Mark written in 69 A.D. 'The Gospel itself is anonymous and is later attributed to John Mark. It is the earliest work to link Jesus' teaching, miracles, travels, death and resurrection in a single narrative.' In 85 A.D. the Gospel of Matthew is written. 'The Gospel itself is anonymous. It is built on the Gospel of Mark but greatly expanded with more teachings of Jesus and added narratives such as the story of Jesus' birth.' The Gospel of Luke and the Acts of the Apostles are written from 85-90 A.D. 'These two works dedicated to a Christian named Theophilus join the stories of Jesus and the early church into one great narrative.' In the years from 90-95 A.D.

the Gospel of John is completed. 'It is based on the distinctive witness of an unnamed "disciple whom Jesus loved", whom tradition has identified as the Apostle John, a son of Zebedee. (John 21:20-24).'(3)

Because the Old Testament was not God's final word one must consider the possibility that the New Testament equally was not God's final word. The Lord's Word is always valid, but it is never final. This is so, this must be so because God is always present. His Presence is not a benevolent observing from a far-off vantage point. His Presence is His Will, His Energy, constantly at work. He is His Presence. He is all in all.

Why then is God's Love so often tied in with conditions in the Bible? Why is God presented as the mighty ruler who judges, who rewards, who punishes, who pardons, who strikes down and who raises up, who offers eternal salvation and eternal damnation? The reason for all this is quite elementary: God had to be presented in a way which was compatible with the spiritual, mental, emotional and even physical capabilities, knowledge and experience of the people of Christ's days.

During these last 2000 years there has been a considerable spiritual development of mankind which, by and large, has kept abreast with the development in the sciences and, on some occasions, has even been helped and accelerated by their achievements. God, through His Presence, has constantly infused His Will into the spiritual development, a fact which is demonstrated by the sadly long list of martyrs in biblical times, and, in more recent times, of Bible translators, reformers and so-called heretics who were persecuted and often met a violent death – officially in the name of the Lord. This spiritual development, created, nurtured and guided by the Lord will one day have progressed to a point where the Lord will decide to manifest Himself on a large scale in a way which is commensurate with the higher spiritual awareness of mankind.

The Old Testament and the New Testament will continue to exist, to be respected and to be treated as His Holy Word. However, it will be realised then that they, by necessity – because of the limitations of human nature – not only revealed the Lord to us, but also concealed the Lord from us when the revelation met the boundary of our capability. This new manifestation of the Lord will not abolish what has been written in the Scriptures, but it will fulfil the Scriptures. This may be in the form of the establishment of His Kingdom on Earth, or the Lord may decide to add to the Scriptures, or the Lord may go well beyond our imagination.

Like the New Testament the New Word of God will establish a new part of the Scriptures. Like the Old Testament and the New Testament, it will be attuned to the people of the day and a certain period afterwards. Like the Old Testament and the New Testament, it will be His Holy Word. Like the Jews who fought tooth and nail to defend 'their' Word of God when Christ appeared and, in the defence of God, did their utmost to stop the Will of God – so will those who believe that the New Testament was the Last Testament defend the Lord and 'their' Word of God in order to stop the Will of God. Like all the other previous Scriptures, the new version of the Lord's Holy Word will not be His Last Word.

(1) The edition of the New Testament in present-day English is called *Good News for Modern Man. The New Testament in today's English Version.* (American Bible Society, 1966).

(2) An example of Christ's Unconditional Love is found in John 9 which relates the healing of the blind man. Christ did not say to him: 'Confess your sins and I will heal you,' or 'Believe in me and I will heal you.' Christ even exposed Himself to the full wrath of the Law when He chose to heal the blind man rather than observe the sabbath.

(3) Quotations in this paragraph from Robinson, Thomas: *The Bible Timeline*.

The Lord on our level

The Lord has to speak to us in our language and at the level of our understanding. When we discuss the Lord, our opinions are expressed in our language and at the level of our understanding. When we argue about the Lord, our categorical statements are in our language and within our understanding. Nothing could be further from the Essence of the Lord than our language and our intelligence.

The church as the body of Christ

It has been said that the church is the body of Christ. If the church is the body, then Christ is the soul. He is the soul which is in a body of people of flesh and blood. He is the soul which constantly counsels the body as effectively as the body allows it to be. As a result, the same relationship exists as within a human being. And the same situation prevails: the spirit is willing, but the flesh is weak. (Matthew 26:41). Therefore we must direct our efforts primarily towards Christ who is One with God and who, at the same time, is One with the Holy Ghost rather than towards the church which is also one with flesh and blood.

The practical situation a believer finds himself in can be complicated by the fact that there is more than one Christian church. In addition, some of these churches do not exist in harmony with each other as the members of the one and only body of Christ should.

Individual churches as well as individual persons may claim that their ideas, their words and their actions are inspired by the Holy Ghost. This may give them more than just peace of mind, but also the sincere conviction that they are the chosen servants of our Heavenly Father and it may fill them with the sense of being on a mission allocated to them by Him. All this makes it very easy to forget that we can do nothing in the name of the Lord unless our own personality moves aside and lets the Lord do it Himself. We must not allow ourselves to make the Lord's plan our own personal plan, to make His Word our own personal word. Quite rightly the question then becomes unavoidable: 'Are we not in a situation where we cannot be sure of anything? Is there no criterion? Are there no guidelines?'

It is actually a wholesome experience to find oneself in such a situation and to realise the daunting nature of one's predicament. This lack of certainty may quite easily lead to apathy, even defeatism. One may then decide to let someone else manage one's own religious affairs. And who could be a better agent for that than a church? As a result, one finds oneself in a very stable framework which stipulates what to think, what to feel, what to say and what to do. All is well then for many people.

Those, on the other hand, who are looking deeper, who are engaged in their own spiritual journey, whose desire to have a personal relationship with the Lord cannot be satisfied within the confines of a church with all its 'do's' and 'don'ts' – those people will find that there is a satisfying solution. Once their personal relationship with God has developed to a certain point, once they have become more aware of God's relationship with them, their faith will lift them above many concerns which disquieten them at the moment. Those present concerns become the future non-issues.

Whenever and wherever the Word of the Lord is preached and implemented, it is done by human beings. This brings the Word of God down to the level of our human understanding. And not only the Lord's

Word, but also the Lord Himself as seen from our point of view.(1) The whole undertaking could be called an exercise in approximation because we just cannot arrive at ultimate values.(2) We must clearly realise that each one of us, irrespective of intelligence of the mind and spiritual growth achieved so far – each one of us has his own level of approximation. It is on this individual level of approximation that the Lord conducts His relationship with each one of 'His children'. This level of approximation is not static, it is never the same, it constantly moves, constantly moves upwards and no matter what height it may reach, it always remains an approximation. Until now this process has been man's experience here on earth.

When the individual is aware of this position on the scale of his spiritual development here on earth he will attempt to see the whole picture. Other individuals and, as a result, the churches as well are in similar situations. Even though there may be an enormous difference between the various individuals and the various churches, each one is in the right position at any particular moment and each one can justify and state this particular position.

All this, however, should be on the understanding that each of these positions is only an approximation. Quite often this understanding is not apparent and, if it does exist, the churches may feel that they cannot afford to adopt it and to preach it. If a church were to include the principle of approximation in its doctrine it would at that very moment abdicate its claim to comprehensive authority. This comprehensive authority is based on the absolute assertion that its teaching is the right teaching and that its organisational structure is the right organisational structure. This situation has been and still is a fundamental predicament of the churches.

With great reverence we preach that Christ was the only man who never sinned, but we, individually and collectively, do not seem to be able to link this with our human existence in thought, in word and in deed. And why not? Simply because Christ was the Son of God and the son of man in the same person. And simply because we, on the other hand, are the sons and daughters of man and are ashamed of our nakedness. We are ashamed of our nakedness which appears as our human imperfection. Adam and Eve stitched fig leaves together in Paradise to hide their nakedness before the Lord because they were aware of it and ashamed of it. We resort to all kinds of measures to hide our human imperfection from our fellow-man because we are ashamed of being human. We even try to hide our imperfection from our innermost selves because we cannot bear to see ourselves as we are. Do we also attempt to hide our nakedness from the Lord? Are we ashamed and afraid of being human even before the Lord? There is no need for all this shame and anxiety before God and before man because we are all His children.

(1)   A North American Indian, Chief White Cloud, once said of his people: 'Earthly things may be argued about with men, but we never argue over God.'

(2)   In *The Universal Dictionary of the English Language* we find the following definition of 'approximation': 'Act of coming near, of becoming almost identical; something which comes near to exact identity, equality, resemblance'.
       In the context of this writing the word 'approximation' has assumed a special meaning. It certainly expresses the process of coming nearer to the objective which is God. However, this movement towards God takes place, as yet, at an immeasurable distance from Him. And, in this world, this drawing near to God will not end at its destination until the Lord wills it. Until then it will remain what it is: a spiritual journey.

The Old Testament and the New Testament today

The religion of the Old Testament, the belief system of the Hebrews, guaranteed salvation. Its more important part was known as the Law which stands for the five Books of Moses. It was up to the believer to observe its demands because his own performance was his stairway to heaven where God was.

For some general information about the law we turn to the glossary of the French Bible. We read that the term 'the Law' is the conventional translation of the Hebrew 'Torah', meaning instruction, directive. First of all it means, as such, all God's commandments for Israel, especially those which Moses established at Mount Sinai. (Exodus 20).

Sometimes the word 'Law' is also used for the books which contain these commandments, that is to say, basically for the first five books of the Bible. The expression 'the Law' subsequently becomes synonymous with 'The Books of Moses', as we read in 2 Corinthians 3:15.

In a still broader sense it means the whole of the Old Testament. (John 10:34). We also come across the expression 'The Law and the Prophets' as an alternative for 'The Old Testament'. In the days of Jesus, we read in the German Bible, 'The Law and the Prophets' was a very common term.

The Apostle Paul sometimes uses the word 'law' to express a force which makes man act, either with good intentions or with evil intentions, as the case may be. (Romans 7:22,23; 8:2).

The stipulations of the Law applied to a wide range of areas: from the structure of the altars, to the rights of Hebrew slaves, to crimes against fellow citizens, to compensation for all kinds of liabilities including property and livestock, to financial dealings, to detailed instructions about religious practices (feasts, sacrifices, ark, table for the bread of the Presence, lampstands, tabernacle, altar for burnt offerings, The Ten Commandments, garments of the priests, offerings for atonement etc.), to different kinds of food, to sexual relationship, to the selection of men for the army, to the order in which the various contingents were to march, to the role of the various houses of the Hebrews, to the inheritance of daughters, to the validity of pledges, to ordinary clothes (e.g. 'You shall make yourself tassels on the four corners of your cloak with which you cover yourself' – 5 Moses 22:12), to the stipulation that a garment be either of wool or of linen but not of both, to tithing, to the requirement that ploughing must not be done with a team consisting of an ox and an ass – the scope and the details of the demands are absolutely astounding. Of special importance were the laws regarding circumcision, the sabbath, purity and purification.

The details and the rigidity of the law went so far that the letter of the law risked killing the spirit of the law. Strong accusations were levelled at Christ, for instance, because He committed the sin of breaking the rules governing the observance of the sabbath: in the eyes of the law He defiled this holy day by healing a blind man. (John 9:14-16).

Since the prophet Ezra (about 450 B.C.) the Law of Moses regulated the whole life of the Jewish people. What we today call a sense of nationhood, of national awareness and pride, became identical with their religion and vice versa. This set the Jews apart from the neighbouring people. It made them inwardly and outwardly God's chosen people.

Then came Jesus. The spiritual revolution. The total revolution. In its magnitude the stark contrast He created must have been almost unbelievable. The teachings and the way of life of the Old Testament were irreconcilable with the spirit of the New Testament. It is no wonder that some ideas and sentiments of the Old Testament found their way into the New Testament. It is not an important point whether it was unavoidable and almost natural under the circumstances, or whether it was an intended concession to the people of the time when the New Testament was written. One could also think that there had to be a certain amount of common ground in particular areas because the New Testament was not only a revolution – a new beginning, but also the next stage of an evolution – a new growing. That was almost 2000 years ago and the circumstances prevailing at that time of transition were so vastly different from the situation today.

The spiritual development achieved by people today who share in a spiritual life has reached a level where the Bible as we know it appears so full of contradictions that one just cannot turn a blind eye to it. One can shrug off these differences, or find some kind of deeper reason for them, or simply become indifferent to them. One can try to believe what the Bible says, but with reservations, concentrating on the parts which obviously are true manifestations of God's Love for us, His children. The people who claim that the Bible, in every detail, is the Word of God find it more and more difficult to sound convincing and to be convincing. Many non-believers, and believers as well, cannot help the feeling that the Bible as a whole was written – or its parts were selected – according to a specific principle: a balance between religion as an uplifting, reassuring blessing and religion as a depressing, destabilising threat. If a believer takes everything he reads in the Bible equally seriously then, at best, he ends up being totally confused. The very serious nature of this confusion and uncertainty is the fact that it is confusion and uncertainty about God, confusion and uncertainty about God's relationship with us, confusion and uncertainty about the very basis and stability of our spiritual lives. As a result, we as individuals are totally affected in our well-being: spiritually, mentally, emotionally and physically.(1) There is a flow-on into our relationship with others in our family and the wider community. In the end this flow-on makes itself felt on a large scale in the whole nation. The decline in moral standards in communities, in whole nations and, indeed, in the whole world has been lamented and criticised. Of course, the difficulties in the areas of faith and religion are not the only aspect of this crisis.

There is little use to continue hammering the teachings of the last 2000 years, because that amounts only to a consolidation of the status quo. In the meantime all kinds of denominations spring up which offer permanent or temporary refuge to those who move away from the longer established branches of the church. More and more people see themselves forced to find their own, personal and uninhibited relationship with God. And how does this situation affect God's relationship with us? It has no bearing at all – nothing ever has – on the everlasting manifestation of God's Unconditional Love.

(1)   In the review of the book titled *When The Soul Cries Out* with the sub-title: *Does Faith Cause Psychological Illness?*, we find the following: 'In many quarters there is discussion of the question – a question which is to be taken seriously – whether the Christian faith makes its followers psychologically ill and unfit for life.' (Neukirchener Kalender 1994, entry for 15-1-1994).

Man is justified by faith and not by his works

All who have sinned without the law will also perish without the law, and all who have sinned under the law will be judged by the law. (Romans 2:12).
. . . so that . . . the whole world may be held accountable to God. (Romans 3:19).(1)

The Law was two things in one: a belief system and the equivalent of our civil and criminal law. In a legal code it may be possible to let one principle argue against another, in which case the questions of interpretation and precedence play an important part. For these reasons the Law lends itself admirably to polemics, to the usage of thoughts and words which manipulate categorical concepts and categorical statements. There is no creative thinking, there is no synthesis, there is only a process of rearranging the units of a preconceived classification. It is like using building blocks: the blocks remain the same, only the configuration changes.

The Pharisees and the Scribes were masters of this art, using the concepts of their religion and also of their worldly law like a chess player uses the figures at his disposal. Each figure was suitable for certain kinds of moves. The total of these figures, combined with the possibilities they represented, made up their game.

They played their game with Jesus, but Jesus did not use their figures.

His concepts were new concepts and new concepts represent new possibilities. Jesus, with His new figures and the new kinds of moves they made possible, completely cut their game to ribbons.

If the Law makes the whole world accountable to God, what practical consequences does that have for us, for example? In plain English this means that each one of us is responsible for his thoughts, feelings, words and deeds. This responsibility presupposes the freedom of choice. A person who does not have the freedom of choice cannot be held responsible for anything he is involved in.

There is no such thing as collective responsibility. There is no possibility that any person or any institution has the right to take over the responsibility for someone else and to impose a particular decision and a particular will on that individual person. Of course, we are talking here strictly about matters of faith and religion.

The distinction must be made between the two. Religion is the body for faith, it is a belief system. Religion is the physical receptacle for faith, its spiritual contents. While there is no body without a soul, there is no religion without faith. When the body dies, the soul lives on forever. When religion crumbles away, faith still lives on forever. As the soul can be without a body, faith can be without a religion.

The circumstances surrounding soul and body are clear-cut. When the soul is without body it has passed over into eternal life. This eternal life is not restricted to the hereafter, it may also take in our earth. The soul may manifest itself to human beings, for instance, only as a voice, or as an apparition before the person's physical eyes.

What then about the situation involving faith and religion? The seat of faith is the soul. A person who has faith is inextricably linked with God, whether he follows a particular type of Christian religion or not. The link is two-fold: firstly, it makes this person one with the God within him; secondly, this God within him, being man's portion of the Lord God Almighty, links him with this same Lord God Almighty.

The term 'accountable' implies, and even demands, some kind of reckoning. Some kind of judgement, some kind of punishment and reward? Judgement at the end of each day, week, month, year? Judgement immediately at the end of a lifetime spent here on earth? Judgement before God in one session for all who have ever been here, a day also known as doomsday, the Last Judgement, the day of wrath?

Christ says that those who believe in Him will pass directly from this life into eternal life. (John 5:24). Paul says that Christ will plead for His faithful as they appear before God to be judged. (Romans 8:34).

If God is the God of Love – indeed, because God is the God of Love and because in itself love is unconditional – there is no judgement. Neither while we are here on earth, nor – and especially not – when our soul has crossed over into eternal life. Since God asks us to love our enemies, would He not 'go there and do likewise'? Since God gave His own Son so that the world be saved, would He not save the souls of His children?

We do have the freedom of choice. Each one of us can read the Bible as we know it and then believe what he needs to believe. In the Bible there are both: there is the God of Unconditional Love and there is the God of 'conditional' love, if there is such a thing as 'conditional' love. There is the God who loves us for what we are: His children. There is the God who loves or disowns us for what we do: struggle in vain to meet all the demands of our religion.

Oh, certainly, faith comes into it and the Grace of God comes into it as well. Since faith is a gift from God, an expression of His Grace, we are actually dealing with the Lord's Grace alone. The Grace of God has two aspects in this context: it can show itself as the granting of faith to any person He may choose; or it can show itself as His pure Grace, just by itself, which is always there for each of His children, irrespective of whether they have been accorded the gift of faith or not.

The Grace of God is not in any way conditional on whether the person is a believer or not. The Lord will not judge a soul, the Lord will not condemn a soul, He will not torment a soul, He will not destroy a soul. In the hereafter there is nothing but eternal life. We have projected our earthly way of thinking beyond our earth, we have shaped the Lord in our human image and we have shaped His Kingdom in the image of the earth.

Why have we done that? Because we want to be able to understand, to dominate with our mind. We have to pray that we learn to think with our God-given souls, learn not to dominate, but to be happy to accept gifts, learn to be happy to become once more a part of the Lord's Creation. Jesus said that we must become children again, inwardly, so that we are able to receive the Kingdom of God.

Was it the Will of God that, in our minds, we fashioned understandable and therefore for us suitable images of the hereafter, of God Himself and His Kingdom? Was it the Will of the Lord that the people of 2000 years ago needed that? Was it the Will of the Lord that the people of those days had reached – and not passed beyond – that particular point along the path of their spiritual development?

The fundamental truth is this: Our soul is our part of God, it is the God in us, like God it is untouchable and eternal. This is the unshakeable beginning and end of any deliberations. Anything else is a meaningless academic exercise.

(1)   Regarding Romans 3:19 : In *The Bible According to Martin Luther's Translation* (in German) and in *The Oecumenical Translation Of The Bible* (in French) instead of the equivalents of the English word 'accountable' we find the respective words for 'guilty'.

The question of righteousness

We say that faith was reckoned to Abraham as righteousness. (Romans 4:9, referring to 1 Moses 15:6).

To find an illustration of the meaning of the word 'righteousness', we may like to look at Matthew 3:13-15. Jesus wished to be baptised by John, but the latter refused initially, saying that it was more fitting that Jesus should baptise him. However, Jesus answered him: 'Let it be so now; for thus it is fitting for us to fulfil all righteousness.' Here the basic idea of the term 'righteousness' is that of conformity with or faithfulness to the Will of God.

God counted Abraham's faith as compliance with His Will which indicates that God considered him as not having sinned. That means effectively that He forgave Abraham that he was human. This is what it amounts to 'since all have sinned and fall short of the Glory of God' as we read in Romans 3:23.

Then Paul points out in verse 24 that the believers in Jesus Christ are justified by His Grace as a gift through the redemption worked by Christ's death on the cross. Then he says that this gift is to be received by faith. In other words, God is gracious, but he bestows His Grace only on those who believe because Christ died only for them. This seems to neglect the fact that, in the biblical sense, man was born a sinner. This is so because God created him that way. On the other hand, we are told that man was born a sinner as a perpetual punishment because of the transgression of Adam and Eve. They were the first humans of our kind here on earth because they were the first sinners.

Paul ties the Grace of God to faith which is His exclusive gift to believers. In this case the Lord is gracious. In the eyes of the non-believer the Lord is not gracious because his sins, his human weakness are not forgiven him. Again, the Lord is presented as a person whose action is not independent, not according to His Will, but whose action is a reaction to what man does. The believer virtually makes a Good God out of the Lord, whereas the non-believer turns God into the God of Wrath.

In fact, God is far above that. The question of righteousness, the need for justification before the Lord are non-issues. They are simply a device to link the concepts and the teachings of the Old Testament with the New Testament. Let us look at the terminology.

> The word 'just' means that the law has been observed, the law as being the expression of the will of a personal or impersonal authority.
>
> In the religious sense 'just' means that the Will of God has been shown loyalty or conformity. In this case the word 'just' is synonymous with the word 'righteous', the former being of Latin origin, the latter coming from an Old English root.
>
> The term 'justification' expresses an action which proves that a person or a fact has been shown to be in keeping with the legal requirements.
>
> In the religious sense a further dimension is added to the word 'justification'. Here it means that the state of a person has been changed from that of a sinner to that of a person 'who has shown loyalty or conformity to the Will of God in thought, word and deed'. Since there is no man who has ever been able to do that consistently, the process of justification quite simply is the forgiving of sins.

Justification comes very close to the notion of purification. In the Old Testament the believers had to purify themselves before they entered the presence of the Lord during worship. Quite unjustifiably, this concept was carried across into the New Testament where it was elevated to the spiritual level. The believer, according to that idea, had to be pure in his inner being as a result of justification, that is having his sins forgiven, before his soul was considered fit to appear before the Lord. This requirement refers to the Last Judgment.

In the Bible there are two lines of opinion about the Last Judgement. Firstly, who believes or believed in Christ will pass directly from life here on earth into eternal life. The second opinion says that Christ will be present at the Last Judgement to vouch for the righteousness of each of the faithful before God the Father. In the latter opinion the forgiveness of sins is verified before the believer is judged by God.

What has happened is the implanting into the new covenant of the spirit of the old covenant which was abandoned by the Lord. Is it an attempt to rehabilitate the Old Testament by diverting some of the life-blood of the New Testament and by adulterating what is left? Is it an attempt to tone down the message of unconditional love of the New Testament because this Divine Love is granted as a gift to all of God's Creation? The Grace of God was granted us long before man existed because His Grace is not an act, but it is part of Him. Because God has always been, His Grace has always been.

Because this grace is available to all and comes without a price, there could have been the fear that, as a result, the precious nature of the Divine Love would not be properly appreciated by the recipients of 2000 years ago and ever since then. Are there not countless people who value any gift and receive it with sincere gratitude? The Unconditional Love from God is treasured by them. This precious gift to them is their lifeline. It is their bond with their Heavenly Father as much as it is the Lord's bond with them. Are they, their relationship with God and God's Unconditional Love for them sacrificed for the sake of those human beings who are different from them? The fear that God's Unconditional Love was not in the best interest of mankind would have found support and direction in Matthew 7:6 where it is written: 'Do not give dogs what is holy; and do not throw your pearls before swine, lest they trample them under foot and turn to attack you.'

Now it is time to stand well back and look at the whole issue and the whole way our thoughts have been flowing. Let us consider the basis of our deliberations.

The soul is immortal, indestructible because it is divine. It cannot be corrupted by the sins of the mind/body part of the human being which is commonly called the flesh. Furthermore, the flesh dies and returns to dust, only the soul survives and enters eternal life.

These facts lead to the following statements:

The question of salvation after death does not exist, there is no basis for it as the soul cannot be blemished.

The concern about man being made righteous before God through his faith has no foundation because man's soul is of God and always in conformity with the Will of God. Man's soul is therefore always righteous.

There is no judgement, neither immediately at the end of a person's life here on earth nor at a special time for mankind collectively. Since only the soul, our portion of God, reaches eternal life, there is no possibility of any judgement.

The believer does not receive preferential consideration over the non-believer. Firstly, because faith is a gift from the Lord. If the Lord in His Wisdom does not grant faith to a particular person during a particular lifetime, He would not punish this person for it. Secondly, the non-believer's soul is also divine, there is absolutely no difference.

Human nature did not come about by accident, it is part of the Lord's Creation. The combination of the spiritual and the physical makes us what we are. Any observer who looks only at the physical aspects of the human being will find that, purely physically, we are like animals: they do neither right nor wrong, they exist. Their whole existence revolves around survival. There is no other concern outside the prime concern: make the utmost of every situation. Any observer who limits his consideration to the purely spiritual qualities of the human being will find that there is an awareness of right or wrong. This, in turn, may lead to the feeling of guilt.

There is no human being who has never done wrong. Whether in each case the wrong is followed by the feeling of guilt and the awareness of sin depends very much on the individual. Discussion whether the Lord would hold the wrong-doing against the individual who is not aware of his actions being sinful or whether He would not count them as sins – this discussion is purely theoretical. The Lord holds nothing against us because He knows us and because He is the God of Love, of Unconditional Love.

It is beyond comprehension that we feel compelled to make ourselves acceptable to God. It is, however, well within comprehension that God accepts us as we are.

The Spirit of the Old Testament is dead . . . long live the Spirit of the Old Testament!

> Note then the kindness and the severity of God: severity toward those who have fallen, but God's kindness to you, provided you continue in his kindness; otherwise you too will be cut off. (Romans 11:22).

Even though Paul himself had declared that man will be saved by faith and not by his own works, he maintains the opposite in this passage. According to him, God's kindness depends on the proviso that we stay within His Kindness. This means effectively that we always listen to the voice of God – to the voice of our soul – and that our mind/body, our flesh, always follows His Counsel. And the alternative? Quite straightforward and stark: otherwise we will be cut off.

Again we are told that our spiritual well-being, our enjoyment of the Unconditional Love of our Heavenly Father, depend on our own effort, our own performance and thus become our own achievement. God's relationship with us is our business, in fact, we turn God into either a severe God or we turn Him into a kind God. Do we have to create God? Are we encouraged to create our own personal God? Does God not have a will of His Own? Is God not His Will? Does the whole situation not remind us of the Old Testament? Does that not remind us of the impossible demand placed on the human being of those days to fulfil the requirements of the Law – or else? Here we have the old theme of the Old Testament expressed in new words in the New Testament. The same tune, only played in a different key.

Paul ignores Isaiah 43:25 where we read: 'I, I am He who blots out your transgressions for my own sake, and I will not remember your sins.'

There are reasons for the extraordinary inconsistency of the Word of God as it is presented in the Bible as we know it. The Bible as we know it is not a statement of faith alone in the sense of a revelation of God the Almighty to His children. If it were, it would be very brief, wonderfully uplifting and divinely inspiring. True, these qualities are there, but woe to the person who turns to the Bible for help and comfort if he opens the Book at an unsuitable page. To read that God regretted having destroyed whatever was on the earth with the great flood (apart from the occupants of the ark) because of man's transgressions – to read that the Lord said in His heart: 'I will never again curse the ground because of man, for the imagination of man's heart is evil from his youth . . .' (Genesis 8:21) – that does not uplift a man's heart when he is desperate for support. Furthermore, it does not fill anybody's heart with hope and confidence when he reads that '. . . God has consigned all men to disobedience, that he may have mercy upon all'. (Romans 11:32). The reader may understand it this way: God has created man incapable of obeying His Will or unwilling to do so which gives Him the opportunity to show His Mercy. Another passage implies that God created man His enemy and that he presumably was His enemy till Christ came into the world: '. . . while we were enemies we were reconciled to God by the death of His Son.' (Romans 5:10). Surely we must credit God with more expertise as a Creator than that. Surely, we must realise that God's Unconditional Love did not suddenly come about and that He decided immediately to send His Son into the world to rectify the situation.

The Bible as we know it is not only a revelation of God the Almighty to His children. It was placed in the hands of the church and remained firmly in the hands of the church till people could read and had access to it. This explains the fact that the early translators of the Bible into modern languages suffered persecution and even death. The Bible was and still is a tool, a guide for living, so to speak, and the church has always felt that it was its God-given prerogative, role and duty to be the administrator and custodian of both the Bible and the believers. Thus the Bible was considered to meet the needs of man, to exercise influence over man's life here on earth and beyond. However, there was and still is by necessity an influence working in the opposite direction as well. What were considered the needs of man, of his human nature, also shaped the Bible, made it suitable for the function it was deemed to carry out. The Bible has been used as a tool ever since it came into being. The nature of a tool allows certain jobs to be done, but, at the same time, the tool is adapted to the jobs at hand.

The Bible as we know it is suitable for anyone in any situation – parts of it. The person who is sensitive, and caring about others and himself, does well to choose what is comforting, uplifting and inspiring. He has to learn to ignore, to treat as non-existent, what is not meant for him. This is not easy and may be fraught with doubt and heartache. It requires a great deal of faith. On the other hand, the person who responds positively to being pushed and confronted with frightening alternatives should ignore what is said about God's Unconditional Love and give heed to what was written for him. It will be easy for him to ignore the words about a Loving God because they do not make sense to him anyway. He will also find it easy to identify with the system of cold-blooded judgement and subsequent reward and punishment.

The Bible is for everyone for various reasons: the Word of God is expressed in our language and at the level of our understanding; the Word of God has also been selected and presented in such a way that it meets certain purposes. Because of this situation the Bible reflects human nature.

Jesus and the Trinity

Jesus has played an important part in the belief of His followers, frequently taking the place of God Himself. However, God does not need Jesus as a go-between and, as a result, we do not depend on Jesus to establish and maintain contact with God. God can deal directly with us, He lives in us, we are His children, there is absolutely no need for His Son – His very Special and Exalted Child – to be our mediator. God was God before He sent Jesus to live among us, God was God in the days of Jesus and He has been and forever will be God.

Jesus did not act on His own behalf, He did the Will of God. Jesus is very similar to us, only on a divine plane: our soul within us is part of God, Jesus is God in His Entirety in a human body. He is God as our fellow-man.

The role of Jesus as a mediator, as a bridge between man and God, is a concession to the limitations of our human understanding. It meets our desire and strong need to comprehend God sufficiently, sufficiently for us. The basis for this understanding and rapport is the dual nature of Jesus: not partly man and partly God, but partly man and entirely God.

Since God had revealed Himself to the people of the Old Testament as God the Father, a suitable name for His Emissary into our world was God the Son. He was also given the name Jesus (as well as Jeshua, Jehoshua in Hebrew and Josua in Greek) which means 'the Lord saves'. In Matthew 1:21 reference is made to this. The Hebrew word 'Messia' presents the Son of God as the Anointed One, as King. It was the tradition in those days to appoint a king by anointing him. The name Christ is derived from Greek, also meaning the Anointed One.

It is quite understandable that the concept of the Trinity had many opponents, such as Paul of Samosata, bishop of Antioch, who was deposed in 272. Not only in the early Christian church do we find sections which do not believe in one God in Three Persons. In our days, there is a Unitarian Church, for example. Unitarianism, which preaches God as One Person, traces its origins to the period of the Protestant Reformation.(1)

The questioning of the trinitarian doctrine may today derive its momentum from the fact that God cannot be likened to a person, that the division of God into God the Father, God the Son and God the Holy Ghost is not compatible with the nature of God. In order to throw a different light on the situation, let us replace 'God' with the word 'Spirit'. The division into God the Father, God the Son and God the Holy Ghost is simply the manifestation of the Spirit in three ways. Manifestation to us, revelation to us, for our purposes – not at all an indication of the nature of the Spirit.

Because Christ said that He is in the Father and the Father is in Him, (2) there is no difference between the two, they are both One. In addition, the Holy Ghost does not remain in isolation either: the Holy Ghost is in the Father and in the Son and both are in the Holy Ghost also. The Father is named after a human concept, the Son is also named after a human concept, which gives both a human aspect, a familiar aspect, and which presents both as persons. Only the Holy Ghost has purely spiritual qualities. Man can only be aware of the existence of the Holy Ghost and believe in It or deny It. He can never claim to be able to accommodate It in his thinking pattern, he can never attach any of his labels to the Holy Ghost.

Today already there is widespread awareness that the Spirit is far above any classification because the Spirit is unique, whereas a classification is derived from a comparison with other phenomena. There is only one Spirit. There are as many names for It as this Spirit has chosen and will choose ways to manifest Itself. There is only One Spirit or, as it says in the Bible, there is only One God. And God is pure Spirit.

In the last 2000 years we have come a long way in our awareness of the Spirit. For instance, we are aware of the Spirit being Its Will, of the Spirit being Its Unconditional Love, of the Spirit being Its Constant Presence, of the Spirit being without beginning and without end, of the Spirit being the only Reality, of the Spirit being the Truth.

(1)   One of those who spoke out against the Trinity was Michael Servetus. He came in contact with some of the leading reformers in Germany and in Switzerland. However, he held views, especially concerning the Trinity, which brought condemnation from the

theologians of the Reformation as well as those of the Catholic Church. He was investigated by the Inquisition, arrested, tried and condemned, but he escaped from prison. When he was travelling from France to Italy, he was arrested on the orders of Calvin, one of the principal reformers. Calvin had founded a government in Geneva based on the subordination of the state to the church. After a long trial in which Calvin's condemnation was a main factor, Servetus was burnt at the stake in Geneva in 1553.

One is very tempted to say that in this case the wheel had turned full circle and the young reformed church had come of age. The reformed church had become an established church. Whoever did not accept its spiritual authority had to be persecuted in the defence of God, His Word and His church.

(2)   Do you not believe that I am in the Father and the Father in me? The words that I say to you I do not speak on my own authority; but the Father who dwells in me does his works. (John 14:10).

Do we really want to have a just God?

When David prays to God for help and deliverance in his Psalms, he does not only submit his pleas. He duly praises Him for His wonderful deeds in the past which to him are proof of His Grace and Favour. God had helped David, but – in order to do that – God had also fought against David's enemies. This fact moves his efforts to survive from a personal level onto a much higher and more general plane: the struggle between David and his enemies becomes the struggle between the righteous and 'those who treacherously plot evil'.(1) The Lord cannot avoid becoming deeply involved in this conflict between good and evil. Being a just God, He must take up the cause of the victim of injustice 'for His Name's sake'. David uses the following words in one of his prayers: 'Bestir thyself, and awake for my right, for my cause, my God and my Lord! Vindicate me, O LORD, my God, according to thy righteousness; and let them not rejoice over me!'(2) In Psalm 63 (verses 9 and 10) David visualises how God will take up his cause, saying: '. . . those who seek to destroy my life shall go down into the depths of the earth; they shall be given over to the power of the sword, they shall be prey for the jackals.'

Not only was David the anointed King of Israel by the Grace of God, but Israel as a whole also had been elevated by God: He had declared it

His chosen people. For this reason the Amalekites who opposed Israel on the way back from Egypt were not merely Israel's enemies, but also God's enemies because they opposed His plans for His people. Therefore the Lord sent Saul on a mission and said: 'Go, utterly destroy the sinners, the Amalekites . . .' All they had was to be utterly destroyed, 'both man and woman, infant and suckling, ox and sheep, camel and ass'. In this case the Lord sends out Israel to punish those who oppose Him and His people. Justice and justification for Israel and absolute supremacy for the Lord in one move.(3)

It is very tempting for us who today pray to God for help, for protection from people and powers who are against us, to follow the pattern we so often see in the Psalms. In the first instance, we appeal to the Kindness and the Love of our Heavenly Father that He may help us in our need. Quite often we also plead our cause, calling on the Lord's sense of justice, pointing out the unfair circumstances we find ourselves in as the result of unfair treatment meted out to us. Then our plea for help combines with equally fervent accusations directed at the origin of our suffering: we appeal for help and we appeal for justice. We ask for our fortunes to be restored and someone's transgressions to be punished. Our cause becomes the Lord's cause since we consider Him to be a just God and therefore ask Him to be a just God.

From a detached and objective point of view one may draw attention to the part of the Lord's Prayer where it says: 'and forgive us our trespasses as we forgive those who trespass against us'. This does not mean that anybody is pointing the finger at the Psalmist or at those of us whose prayers for help follow his example.

When we call on the Lord for help, our words should not ask for more, only for help. This kind of prayer keeps our case on a personal level with God, on a one-to-one level. This way our words appeal to God's Love only.

Our need may vary in nature: it may concern merely us as individuals, it may involve our fellow-man, we may not be responsible for our own need, we may be responsible for someone else's need. In each and every case we do well to ask the Lord for help, appealing to His Unconditional Love.

Because of the imperfection of our human nature and the physical nature of the world we live in, we cannot avoid doing wrong. If we clamour for justice today in the role of the plaintiff, we can be sure that somebody else will clamour for justice some time in the future, putting us in the position of the defendant. Therefore it is not in anybody's long-term interest to have a just God. If we as human beings ask for justice, we will ultimately be found guilty.

In the Old Testament the God of Unconditional Love would have been totally out of place. Could He have helped Israel to drive out the Canaanites and other nations so that He could give their land to His chosen people?(4) Could a God of Unconditional Love have proclaimed laws which called for punishments ranging from compensation (2 Moses 21:18,19), to sin offering (3 Moses 4:1-3), to beating (5 Moses 25:1-3), to ransom (2 Moses 21:30), to the cutting-off of the offender's hand (5 Moses 25:11,12), to stoning (5 Moses 17:1-7; 21:18-21; 22:20,21), to burning (3 Moses 20:14) and to hanging (5 Moses 21:22,23)? God had to be a just God because He had to establish laws. It is in the very nature of laws that they apply to those who keep them and to those who break them. The ultimate purpose of punishment was '. . . you shall purge the evil from your midst; and all Israel shall hear, and fear'.(5) The principle had to be that the punishment fitted the crime. This point is vigorously demonstrated by the following quotation: '. . . I the LORD your God am a jealous God, visiting the iniquity of the fathers upon the children to the third and the fourth generation of those who hate me' – this is then balanced with 'but showing steadfast love to thousands of those who love me and keep my commandments'.(6) Indeed, punishment and reward delivered by a just God.

Even though the force of the law is directed specifically at the offender, the effects of the punishment are not restricted to that person. He has relatives and friends who would be affected because they would share the trauma and the shame. However, it is one thing to punish a person, but it is another thing to continue to punish the three or four following generations as well. This kind of punishment is again stipulated in 5 Moses 5:9.

The instances quoted so far in this chapter do not represent isolated situations. In 2 Samuel 24:10-17 we read that, after having sinned, David prayed to the Lord asking: 'take away the iniquity of thy servant; for I have done very foolishly'. However, God rejected David's plea and offered him the choice between three kinds of punishment: three years of famine, or three months of being pursued by his enemies, or three days of pestilence in his land. David did not choose, but decided that he and his people should let themselves 'fall into the hand of the LORD, for his mercy is great'. The Lord sent a pestilence upon Israel which killed seventy thousand men. A whole nation was punished for the transgression of one person.

Justice, especially at its most severe, becomes injustice for the innocent who are also involved against their will. Is this collective punishment motivated by the desire for revenge? Is it intended to teach a lesson? Is it simply a powerful display of the supreme independence of a God who says: 'I will be gracious to whom I will be gracious, and I will show mercy on whom I will show mercy'.(7) To which is added in Romans 9:16 'So it depends not on man's will or exertion, but upon God's mercy.' And this mercy appears – in the examples given so far in this chapter – to be based solely on God's Will which does not necessarily take into consideration whether or not it adversely affects people who love Him and keep His Commandments.

Punishment directed at the offender and collective punishment which involved persons who were not at all connected with the crime obviously were standard procedure to the people of those days. Did not the crowd shout that the blood of Jesus be on them and on their children after Pilate had tried in vain to set Jesus free instead of Barabbas.(8)

Had God decided to go to such lengths with punishment and reward to demonstrate His Absolute Authority? Was He intent on showing His Power and His Glory to the people of the Old Testament in ways which they understood? Did He come down to their human level to manifest Himself in their terms in order to be understood? Is it a characteristic feature of the Old Testament that God comes down to man's level and behaves like a human being in order to be understood? It appears that He not only spoke the language of man, but that He also acted and reacted like man.

If this was the case, or if it appears to us to have been the case, then we are in the happy position to say that the trend has been reversed. Since the appearance of Christ the process of God and man coming closer together has, by the Grace of God, moved along a new path. God has reached down to our level and is now lifting us up towards Himself. Ever so gently and ever so slowly as seen from an absolute point of view, but very noticeably and quite quickly according to our perception and experience.

And how is this happening? It is the process of the Lord establishing His Kingdom. He is establishing the Kingdom which is within. Within whom or what? Within us. He is already there, He has been there for a long time, He has always been there. In our souls. Not precisely in our souls, but as our souls. His Presence is now becoming reality for us, increasingly so. Reality for us is directly proportionate to our perception, to our ability to perceive. By the Grace of God, our perception of His Presence has increased in a wonderful way: through the growing awareness of the divine nature of our soul. The Lord has been working miraculous changes within us human beings by raising our vibrations – just to mention one way which we can perceive and somewhat understand. Much of the change we can be aware of only through intuition or revelation. We need not understand everything, we need not even be aware of everything, we do not even have to know everything in our hearts, we do not even have to know in detail what we believe. Faith does not depend on knowledge and understanding. The Will of God is at work.(9) It has always been so, but now it is becoming more and more obvious. The Will of God is being seen to be at work.

Our present spiritual life contrasts so marvellously with the spiritual situation which the people of the Old Testament were locked into. Their whole life was governed by the kind of God He chose to be for them. In His man-like role the God of Israel was the God, who – though invisible – spoke the language of man, acted and reacted like a human being. He was the God who established the law, watched over its observance, punished and rewarded: He was the God who played the role of a father, He was God the Father.

Then God the Father appointed His Successor, His Son Jesus Christ. Not just another manifestation of God, not just a new generation of God. The hitherto invisible God, the God whose sight was fatal to man, the God who came face to face with His servant Moses – now, as Christ, assumed a physical appearance which was visible and accessible to all. God the Father's relationship with Israel was widened by Christ to embrace all mankind. Christ did not sit in judgement like His Father. He preached the forgiveness of sin, He Himself forgave sins, He Himself gave His Life for us so that we should all know that our sins are forgiven. He did not break any man's body, mind, or soul – He healed them, He just healed them. His Love was not the Love of a just God who, as such, had to love the one and hate the other. Since He never sat in judgement, He did not have to be a just God: His Love could be Unconditional Love. His Supreme Sacrifice is there to be seen by all and to be believed by all: the ultimate act of His Unconditional Love.

One may be inclined to say that we have digressed, that we have strayed from the topic, but we have not. We have simply allowed 'our' thoughts to run their course. Their direction and their contents arise quite naturally out of themselves. This is their way of being true. True to themselves, in fact.

Now let us return to the initial area of our considerations. As we have seen, bringing the offender to justice also means bringing compassion and protection to the rest of the people. Some groups who were given special attention were the Hebrew slaves, the poor, the hired servants, sojourners, widows and orphans. The law-abiding citizen of Israel enjoyed the protection of the law as his just reward. He was entitled to God's Love which was the Love of a just God. God Himself had to observe the law which he had established for His people.(10) As a just God He had to reward the one and punish the other, He had to love the one and hate the other.

The God of the Old Testament certainly had His place in the Old Testament. He entirely and definitely belongs there and nowhere else since Christ's teaching and His sacrifice on behalf of us all.

As for our worldly affairs, we must keep in mind the fundamental difference between the times of the Old Testament and our time. Before Christ there was only one law and that was the Law of the Five Books of Moses. It was a blend of religious doctrine and worldly government, of the spiritual and the physical. For quite some time now worldly affairs have been subject to laws which are the domain of worldly institutions. Spiritual guidance still has access to these laws. Ideally, it can influence them via the spiritual attitude of every person who has the opportunity to make his voice heard and his opinion be counted. There are the legislative and executive branches of government which take care of worldly matters, quite separate from the churches which attend to spiritual concerns.

There simply is no place in our lives for a just God because justice excludes unconditional love. Since we know that God is Unconditional Love, justice excludes the God we know.

Let us conclude with the wonderful words of the Apostle John which are recorded in chapter 1 verses 14 and 17: 'And the Word became flesh and dwelt among us, full of grace and truth . . . And from his fulness have we all received, grace upon grace. For the law was given through Moses; grace and truth came through Jesus Christ.'

(1)   Psalm 59:5
(2)   Psalm 35:23,24

(3)   1 Samuel 15:1-3,18
(4)   Joshua 3:10
(5)   5 Moses 21:21
(6)   2 Moses 20:5,6
(7)   2 Moses 33:19
(8)   Matthew 27:25
(9)   . . . God is at work in you, both to will and to work for his good pleasure. (Philippians 2:13).
(10   While the ark of God was being taken from the house of Abinadab to Jerusalem, the oxen pulling the cart stumbled. Uzzah, one of Abinadab's sons, put out his hand to the ark and took hold of it to prevent it from toppling over. And the Lord in his anger smote Uzzah there and then because he touched the ark. He was punished for having shown contempt* for the Law which allowed only Levites to touch the ark and he was not a Levite.
*The French Bible uses the word 'insolence' to describe Uzzah's behaviour. (2 Samuel 6:1-7).

Where two or three are gathered in My Name . . .

. . . where two or three are gathered in my name, there am I in the midst of them. (Matthew 18:20).

This quotation refers to the coming together of two or more people who invoke the Presence of the Lord. It is their wish and prayer that He may be present, that He may sanctify their togetherness and that He may fill each one of them with His Holy Ghost. It is a conscious act of worship, it is a conscious experience of the Lord's Presence.

One may wonder whether the Lord's Presence depends exclusively on the express desire of those who are together, or whether the Lord is with them already in one way or another. The answer to this question is close at hand. It is the practical experience of many people who are attuned to the spiritual emanations coming from the souls of their fellow-men that their togetherness assumes the qualities of fellowship. This kind of fellowship, this kind of spiritual awareness, this kind of communion without explicit expression, this kind of experiencing the Presence of the all-embracing Divine Spirit – this kind of fellowship may have been the prerogative of religious occasions in the past. If this was the case, then times have changed, to use a well-worn phrase. This cliche, however, is hollow, meaningless and only blurs the picture. Times have not changed, but people have made tremendous progress along the path of their spiritual journey. Since we know and since we are quite familiar with the fact that God is within us,(1) that our soul is our portion of God,(2) we readily understand. It is an understanding which will remain an understanding within the heart, it will not be an understanding based on the results of a vivisection carried out with the stainless steel scalpel of the insensitive mind. It is correct to say that the experience of the Divine Spirit brought about by the company of others is a spontaneous manifestation of the Divine Spirit. A manifestation which does not assume and does not need the fixed form and presentation of religious ceremonials. Quite simply: the God in one person speaks with the God in another person in His Own Way.

One may also wonder about the Lord's Presence when there is only one person involved. In this case also the answer already exists before the question is thought of. The vibrations of the person's soul do not represent a detached and self-contained phenomenon, they are not an isolated part among other isolated parts. Far from it. Like the simultaneous spiritual experience of a group of people, the individual person's vibrations are an extension, a part of the harmony which pervades the universe – the harmony of vibrations which is the Oneness of the Divine Creation. In the vastness of this Divine Creation each one of us has his place and plays his part within the Presence of God: this God speaks in His Own Way with the God in the individual person.

(1)   Ephesians 4:6
(2)   Psalm 73:26

The God within us and the God around us

It must be pointed out that we use contradictory terms when we speak of the God within a human being as being separate from the God who is the Divine Energy of His Creation. To make a distinction between the two, as we did in the preceding chapter 'Where two or three are gathered in My Name . . .' was a temporary step which helped us to understand. Now that we have gained understanding, we can and we must discard completely any thought of there being more than one God, or parts of Him being distinguishable from the whole. No matter what manifestations there are of Him, no matter how many notions we have of Him, no matter how many names and words are trying to capture Him, He is one and the same: He is the Oneness. And the term 'Oneness' represents once more a vain attempt which will not take us further than a limited degree of awareness as we may find when we read John 17:20-23.

Where to, freedom of thought?

There is the concept of freedom of thought which generally refers to the fact that a person has the opportunity to think whenever he wishes and whatever he wishes. This is what we may call the external freedom of thought. However, there is also what we may call the internal freedom of thought.

Whereas the term external freedom of thought refers to the circumstances surrounding the person, the expression 'internal freedom of thought' refers to the conditions prevailing within the person. There must be freedom within the person, freedom for the thoughts to develop according to their innate qualities. This means that – on the part of the person's mind – there must not be any preconceived ideas, consciously or subconsciously, about the direction his thoughts should take, what they should be focussing on and what results they are expected to bring. In other words, the person must not be in charge of his thinking. Thinking must be completely free, completely independent in order to fulfil its own innate purpose to its own satisfaction.

This very special state within a person cannot be created at will, it is and has to be the result of a development, of self-development. Again our thoughts are turned, actually 'they turn themselves', towards the concept of vibrations. When a person's vibrations reach a certain frequency, then the person's will – the hallmark of his ego – can glide into a state of suspended animation. It is so often our will which gets in our way, literally steering our change in a direction where it cannot be development, but is destined, at best, to remain a change only. Our will may even be so strong and fixed that it will prevent even change, a situation which has the potential to become the starting point of self-destruction.

The state when the person's will is in suspended animation we may also call an altered state of consciousness. In such a condition the person is ready to be integrated into the spiritual energy which surrounds each one of us, as individuals separately and as mankind collectively.(1) In fact, because this state of being spiritually integrated separately and collectively exists at the same time – one process being superimposed on the other – there is no possibility of telling one from the other. The complete elimination of any possibility of differentiation is the characteristic of oneness. As far as we are concerned, there is and can only be one unique oneness and that is the Oneness of the Spirit.

Our participation in this Oneness, our being part of this Oneness, does not transfigure us into angel-like beings; this is reserved for the hereafter. Being part of this Oneness, on the other hand, does present us the opportunity to move and to grow towards the Spirit.

It is an uplifting experience to become aware of the suspended animation of one's very own will and of one's very own logic: to be already part of the Oneness and, at the same time, to be moving and to be growing towards It. This process is endless within itself and it cannot be terminated through outside interference. Furthermore, it is a development which, within itself, is its own fulfilment. It is at once movement and place. As such, it does not have an end, but it also has not had and never has a beginning. It is part of the all-embracing Oneness which is also known as 'I am'.

(1)   We have for a long time had a word for this phenomenon: inspiration. It is derived from the Latin word 'spirare' meaning 'to breathe'. The word 'spirit' comes from the same verb. In other words, the Spirit breathes into the person. Are we not reminded of the creation of Adam when God breathed life into him? This giving of life, this giving of Spirit, is available to us here and now and throughout our lives.

The Word of God as we know it

The Word of God as we find it in today's Bible is the main source of our knowledge of God. It imparts to us the basis for our belief system which we commonly call our religion. In many cases this belief system functions like the skeleton functions for the body: it provides the structure, the possibilities for a person's faith with regard to depth, strength, enthusiasm and resilience.

And yet, the Word of God as we find it in today's Bible, when looked at closely, consists of two elements like any kind of language: form and content. The form is decidedly either compatible with the human being, or it is of human origin. The content is of Divine Nature and of Divine Origin.

The form of this communication between God and us, His children, consists of language patterns which are so arranged that they convey the knowledge of God. These language patterns may have been well-tried and well-used over a certain time, or they may be entirely new ones which are specifically devised to express a hitherto unknown facet of God, or to describe Him from a new point of view. Thus God manifests Himself through the medium of human language.

What implications does the use of a human language have for the communication from God? How can the Divine content form a harmonious combination with the form of a human language? The Divine content is certainly powerful enough to mould the existing language to suit its purpose, but it still remains a human language.

We must remember that a human language is the thinking pattern of its speakers. Therefore we must say that God uses a human language so that we hear familiar sounds, see familiar writing and think within the limits of our mental capacity. The span and depth of our knowledge of God is identical with the capacity of our words and our thoughts. No preacher has therefore the right to say that what he considers to be the Word of God is the absolute and final knowledge we can have of God. Nobody, no matter how learned or eloquent he may be, is justified in saying that what he preaches is right and anything which is different is wrong.

The Lord has been so gracious to us, to bow down so low, to speak to us so lovingly, to speak to us as we would speak to a little child. In His Kindness He speaks to us about things which we, as His little children, can understand. He speaks about things which to us, His children, are so comforting, so reassuring, so uplifting, so joyful, so promising and so very, very important.

For those of His little children who may think that they have heard and understood as much as He is able to say there is a gentle reminder in Isaiah 55:8 which reads: '. . . my thoughts are not your thoughts, neither are your ways my ways, says the LORD.'

Undonditional love in our present belief system

We may well ask the question why unconditional love in our traditional religious teaching applies only to the human being and why we find it difficult or even impossible to accommodate it with God.

When the Bible demands from us that we love our enemies,(1) a considerable amount of activity has to take place to clear the way for love. First, the past with all its animosity has to be eliminated. Then, the present with all its very acute ill-feelings and their well-founded reasons has to be overcome. Most likely there is already some forward planning for the contingencies which might arise from the present enmity. These plans also have to be dismantled in our hearts and in our minds. Our mind may tell us that such undertakings are likely to threaten our very existence, that all this is definitely so absurd. Will altruistic thinking give us the strength to change course? Will unquestioning faith give us the strength to ignore the past? Will both combine to make it possible? To achieve this, even in the best of circumstances, is an enormous task for the average human being who is so tied in with his physical nature and his physical surroundings that – as somebody put it – he cannot live for more than three hours without thinking of food. A wide canyon can open up between the demand 'you shall' and the realistic and tangible situations of our daily lives.

Of course, the demand that one should love one's enemies, that one should love one's neighbour as one loves oneself(2) – this demand has been met and happily accepted by many as a guiding principle. Not only believers belonging to various religions, but also so-called atheists have acted in its spirit.

One must wonder whether God, as He is presented in the Bible as we know it, established these demands, these commandments, exclusively for us as guidance because we need them. Nevertheless, it is somewhat surprising that God did not make statements about Himself which match the simplicity and directness of the principles which He laid down for man. It can be a little bewildering that we read in the Bible statements about God's unconditional love, then about His love which is restricted to certain people under certain conditions and then about His straight-out condemnation and annihilation of others. One must wonder whether God's official attitude to man has to vary as much as human nature varies – from unconditional love to merciless judgment – because He had to deal with each individual occurrence in man's life on its separate merits. Within our understanding of God, there has been really no possibility for Him to be the God of Love only. Nor has there been the possibility for Him to be the God of Wrath only. And yet, He had to be the one God. Fortunately for us, this oneness was achieved in the concept of the just God.

111

Man was happy to have a just God because He is the mirror image of the kind of human beings we are. We simply have to have a God with personality, with a personality which we comprehend, which acts and reacts in a way which we understand. And beyond our understanding, an immeasurable distance beyond our understanding, lies the God who is Truth. The only way for us to break out of the confines of our idea of a 'man-like' God is for us to receive the Grace of God which will increase the awareness of His Presence within us.

His increasingly perceptible Presence within us will make it increasingly possible for us to think absurd thoughts and make decisions which defy logic, something which is the outward sign of following the guidance of unconditional love. In this way, we think with our heart. Or, more appropriately, our mind listens to our heart. Or, to present the actual fact, the Presence of the Lord in our soul merges with the human element of our mind to produce the Oneness which the human being has been longing for since time immemorial.

(1)   Matthew 5:44
(2)   3 Moses 19:18

Is Christ the personification of Divine Unconditional Love?

In word and deed, Christ presented Himself as the obedient Son of His Heavenly Father and yet, on occasions, He broke the Law. He broke the letter of the Law in order to respect the spirit of the Law. For instance, He did not forbid His disciples to strip some ears of grain while they were walking through a field on a sabbath because they were hungry. As a result, He was promptly accused by the Pharisees of allowing the sabbath to be profaned because harvesting was not permitted on the sabbath.(1) In the minds of the Pharisees He again came into conflict with the Law when He healed a man who had been blind since birth.(2) This was a grave sin because healing was allowed on a sabbath only if a person's life was at risk. Like everybody else, Christ knew that violating the sabbath was often punishable by death.(3) In this case, Christ showed again that He was and is above the Law. With Christ, we see for the first time that God is above the Law and that He is and that He acts in accordance with Himself.

Now let us look at a hypothetical situation. Suppose that Christ came back into this world again as Christ and that it would happen in our lifetime. Suppose that He would again act out His Unconditional Love as He did in His first appearance here on earth, from His miracles to His death on the cross. Suppose that He would follow up His actions by formulating a belief system which fully captures the spirit of His actions: Unconditional Love. Suppose His disciples would then rewrite the New Testament in this very same spirit. Can anybody imagine the difference it would make to the New Testament; the difference it would make to the spiritual situation of the believers and the present non-believers; the difference it would make to the religious organisations of all denominations? Perhaps nobody can. However, everybody can imagine that the difference would range from miraculous to catastrophic. Christ would indeed make everything new – and we have been told that He would do just that after His second coming.

Then the words 'Peace on Earth' will become 'Unconditional Love on Earth'.

And the Lord will write these words on the heart of every one of His children; not as a law, but as a sign that the heart is filled with His Presence. And no one will have to teach his fellow-man, saying: 'Look, brother . . . listen, sister, such is the Will of the Lord.' Every one of us will know no alternative to the Will of the Lord, which is His Unconditional Love, which is the Lord Himself. And this will be the perfect Oneness with the Lord, which is His Kingdom on Earth.

(1)   Mark 2:23-28
(2)   John 9
(3)   4 Moses 15:32-36

Conclusion

To place what we have just finished reading in its broader context, we may do well to remind ourselves of the purpose of this writing.

There is no purpose in this writing other than to state what had to be said.

It was written for its own sake.

It does not present itself as a tool to be used because a tool can be used in so many ways for so many different purposes, some of which may serve the interests of the user only. It is not a ways and means for someone's plans and ambitions.

This writing does not present the writer's personal thoughts. He merely wrote down what was given to him.

This writing as such does not consider itself to be antagonistic to ideas from which it differs. It is not hostile either to institutions which are based on these ideas. It does not criticise. It does not judge. It is not concerned with other ideas and other concepts. It does not tell anybody what to do and what not to do. It is simply there.

A person's acceptance or non-acceptance of what is stated in this writing is entirely his choice. If somebody decides to ignore it, that again is entirely his choice. To make a choice is to exercise one's freedom.

Finally, the writer wishes to describe his own experience in the hope that his comments may be helpful.

While he has been making his journey through this writing, the reader will have noticed that he came across certain statements which differed from what had been said previously. Not only may there have been variations, but there may have been such a contrast that subsequent statements superseded earlier details.

This was certainly not the intention of the writer as he was not and is not in a position to have intentions with regard to this writing. What he was to write was given to him in a very special way. He was granted the wonderful privilege to journey along with the ideas as they evolved. He was never tempted nor was he ever able to rush ahead because he had no prior knowledge of what lay in front of him. He was being taught as he wrote. His understanding quite often lagged behind, but this was not of any consequence because the writing was not of his own doing. The demands on his understanding gradually increased as his understanding was made to grow. The concessions to his limited understanding were earlier much greater than later on, which appears to be the main reason for certain aspects to be presented differently at a later stage.

The question of right or wrong is not appropriate because none of the statements claims to be a statement of absolute and permanent validity. There cannot be absolute and permanent validity where our thinking, our language, our understanding are involved. And yet, within these our limitations, there is a wonderful scope for change, for development, for a humble and grateful sense of achievement, for joy and happiness thanks to the Grace of God and His Unconditional Love.

P.S. Some time after the completion of the manuscript a message was received that the contents of this writing can be summed up in one sentence:

'God is a God of Unconditional Love.'

PART TWO

FOREWORD

In August 1995 one had the impression that the then manuscript – now Part One – was a well-rounded and complete piece of writing. However, a few months later, it became obvious that this was not so.

Part Two presents further development of earlier ideas with varying results. Firstly, existing ideas may be brought to a conclusion, if one may be so bold as to say so. On the other hand, the continued unfolding of a topic can head in a new direction, establishing itself as something different. Its new character may be so pronounced that it contradicts certain points which were made earlier, making them entirely redundant.

This development does not take anything away from the importance the superseded concepts had when they were introduced. They were necessary stages of growth which, once outgrown, had outlived their purpose. To be alive in the complete sense of the word is to be in a constant state of becoming which embraces a blend of acquiring, of absorbing, of reworking, of discarding. It is reassuring to see that this fundamental principle has been at work in this writing.

Acknowledgments

During the writing of this section several more good friends played an important part. The location of a suitable publisher was the result of Elsie and Jackie's help. I am much obliged to Margaret, a friend from a previous lifetime, and to Domenico, a very special friend, for their wonderful support. Martie's work with the computer has also been much appreciated. I am also very grateful to Graeme for providing much needed assistance in the closing stages. Finally I would like to thank Regency Press for being so helpful with this publication over such a lengthy period of time.

Australia,
January 1999

God does not change

In a television series presented by a Jewish rabbi a Christian clergyman was interviewed. The latter made a very reassuring comment about God.

He said that God is Love. He forgives us our sins. We think that in one instance He forgives sins and in another He does not. That is not a correct observation. God does not change. The change is within us. Consider that the sun is shining through my window. If I draw the curtain the sun does not come in. If I decide to be in darkness that is possible for me to do, but I cannot stop the sun from shining.

Which way at the crossroads?

It is very difficult for many people not to think about God and, as a result, not to talk about Him. We have a need to express what we think about Him, what we feel about Him, how to experience Him within us and in the world around us. To put this experience into words helps us to become more and more aware of His Presence and to continue to advance in His direction.

Since I am not the only person who thinks and talks about God, my opinions find themselves side by side with the opinions expressed by other people.

This means that I have reached the crossroads. Before I proceed any further, I have to ask myself one decisive question: 'Do my thoughts and conclusions concerning God have a tendency to compete with the ideas of others?' If the answer is in the affirmative, I am setting out on a road which leads into the spiritual wilderness.

It is not I who decides to take this road, but my ideas. There is not just one decision, but a whole chain of decisions because one idea leads to another. I simply go along with my ideas; what else can I do? First I notice that my ideas compare favourably with the ideas of others, therefore mine must be better. Then enthusiasm and devotion combine spontaneously to enlist in the services of the good cause. Yes, they do. Even if there were no good cause, they would create one because they absolutely need one. The good cause is God. Not any God, certainly not. One serves wholeheartedly and sincerely only the God one believes in. Therefore it must be the kind of God who is presented in a way I can identify with. He is then my God and my King.

It is not long before I find myself in the public arena where all sorts of religious doctrines either embrace each other or growl and hiss at each other. Surely, I cannot stand idly by and not speak up in the defence of my God and His Word. And when all the noise has died down and the dust has settled it becomes so obvious to me that I am called upon – even chosen – to dispel the various misconceptions about my God, the true God.

To begin with, I must try hard to convince others that they are in error and I must work hard to convert them. If need be, I must send in my ideas to do battle with opposing opinions.

Since I identify with my ideas, I cannot help feeling personally attacked when they are being belittled or found fault with. Of course, the best defence is to attack in return. We all have to fight the good fight for the Prince of Peace. That has been the tradition for centuries. And what has this tradition led to? Personal enmity, even within families. Divided communities. Devastation. Untold tragedies. Even full-scale religious wars. And religious wars are the most horrendous aspect of the spiritual wilderness.

Having realised that we cannot go astray any further, we decide to go back to the crossroads. The other direction offers itself as the way out of our dilemma. It is a new direction for many; it is a new approach which many established churches will be ill-equipped to embrace. Rather drastic groundwork has to be done in order to take away the basis for the attitudes of the past, in order to clean up the breeding grounds of so many problems.

In certain respects we have been captives of some religious doctrines which now have little more than historical value. They tell us what was appropriate centuries ago, completely ignoring the spiritual progress man has made in the meantime. These doctrines have survived because they were cast in a certain kind of language which was updated only in vocabulary, spelling and pronunciation, but not in thought content.

The concept of 'God' is an important case in point. The God in Three

Persons is an idea which leads into the spiritual wilderness. To establish this idea was a deft move to prevent the early Christian church from worshipping three separate gods. When we speak of God the Father, God the Son and God the Holy Ghost we now realise that they are manifestations of The One which were made to man at his level of understanding.

The concept of The One gives us the new direction which will allow us to avoid the pitfalls and dead-ends of the past. We can be perfectly comfortable with the realisation that when we put forward ideas about The One, we only express our point of view. We can be quite content in the knowledge that our ideas can never capture the Essence of The One. Furthermore, we can be assured that we are not in a fixed position opposite the unchanging image of a Spirit. Rather, we are on earth to enjoy a spiritual journey of a special nature:

> our progress along our spiritual path is always right for us, the individual;
> all human beings are on individual journeys which may be identical, similar, or different;
> each spiritual journey is a journey without end because we never cease to progress, we never arrive at a destination and the opportunities for spiritual growth are limitless;
> the essence of the spiritual journey is the increasing awareness of The One;
> here on earth the increasing awareness of The One will always be an approximation;
> there is an individual approximation for each individual person at any given moment;
> therefore each person has a direct relationship with The One;
> to have this direct relationship with The One is the divine right of each individual;
> this divine right of the individual is as absolute as the individual's soul itself.

Our awareness of the special aspects of our spiritual existence on this earth is creating a new spiritual climate. We have been longing for this development although we were not able to say even in our hearts what we were waiting for. Admittedly, the future does not lie in front of us like an open book, but one thing we know quite clearly: we are on a personal journey of discovery.

The One and manifestations of The One

In the Bible as we know it we read of God the Father, God the Son and God the Holy Ghost. We are told furthermore that God is a God in Three Persons: the Father, the Son and the Holy Ghost.

It is interesting to note that the Father and the Son, because of the names they have, are easy to imagine as persons. To see the Holy Ghost personified is very surprising because we cannot give the Holy Ghost a word, a name, which is derived from a person. It is quite obvious that the Holy Ghost, the concept of the Holy Ghost, presents a difficulty of definition.

When we define something we say what it is and, by doing so, outline its boundaries. We actually say where it ends, as the word 'define' comes from the Latin word 'definire' which in its basic meaning translates as: 'to set the bounds or limits of something'. In other words, we literally attempt the impossible; we attempt to circumscribe the Holy Ghost. We try to draw an imaginary line around the perimeter of the Holy Ghost. This imaginary line consists of words and the words are the expressions of thoughts. With our thoughts and with our words we stipulate what the Holy Ghost is and what it is not. Are we aware that we actually create the Holy Ghost at our human level of intelligence? Do we do this so that we can be comfortable with the concept of the Holy Ghost? Do we do this because we cannot be comfortable with something which is outside our range of perception? Do we do this because of the urge – the necessity even – to dominate, to have power over the world around us?

Since we must dominate the world around us physically, we change it to suit our abilities and, above all, our inabilities. And if we cannot dominate the world around us physically, we dominate it mentally: we change it from what it really is to what we think it must be to suit our abilities and, above all, our inabilities.

We have created a world for us which consists of illusions and God is part of this world. We have made each other believe what we thought was profound wisdom and we have ended up with a world of make-believe and God is part of this world. The irony of it all is that there is nothing wrong with this because that is all we as human beings are capable of doing. The tragedy of it all is that we give the results of our activities the hallmark of unquestionable reality. Our illusions we proclaim to ourselves and to others to be the truth – the unquestionable truth.

This takes us a step further. The nature of the truth is that it is unique, that there is no other truth beside the truth. Thus we effectively maintain that there is no other truth beside our truth. As a result, we deliberate, discuss, argue, quarrel, fight with words and with swords – instead of assessing where we stand and why we find ourselves in such a position.

The magic word is 'self-denial'. Its wholesome properties are released only by its correct use. It can be used wrongly to mean that one is utterly incapable, insignificant and not worthy to be of any concern to one's fellow-man and especially not to God. In other words, to use self-denial in the wrong sense means to destroy oneself. In the positive sense self-denial makes us realise that we are part of God's Creation, that physically and mentally we have a beginning and an end, that we cannot be a law unto ourselves, that we are an integral part of a big plan. When we have reached this point, we can discard the word 'self-denial' – which means 'saying 'no' to oneself' – and replace it with the positive and so constructive notion of humility.

As humble human beings we are assured of the right attitude, the right approach, the ability to be accepting, the ability to receive gratefully, the ability to integrate ourselves gracefully. Now the scales have fallen from our eyes. Now we hear more than just the sound of our voices. Now we are happy to perceive what we are able to perceive within our limitations. Now there is no need to assert ourselves. Bewildering and constantly escalating complexity has changed to refreshing simplicity.

Now we can stand back and listen and observe. The Holy Trinity of God the Father, God the Son and God the Holy Ghost is a concept which we can understand more or less. It is in fact a concession to our limited human understanding. As such, this concept invites interpretation, leading to the kind of differences which have marred our spiritual lives. In reality, the situation is straightforward. The three persons, the God in Three Persons, are three manifestations of a higher Entity which we best call 'The One'. These three manifestations of The One are, by necessity, different from The One. There is nothing beside The One. And The One is the Truth. And there is nothing beside the Truth.

We can actually visualise an ascending line from mankind to God the Son, then to God the Father, continuing to God the Holy Ghost and then, beyond, towards The One. In reverse we can say that The One manifested as the Holy Ghost and God the Father on the divine level. Then The One manifested on the combined divine and human level as

God the Son, Jesus Christ. However, this is not all.

Then The One manifested on the purely human level as mankind. This idea may appear to be surprising, but the situation is actually obvious. Each and every one of us has a soul which existed before we entered this world and which will continue to exist after we have left this world. Our soul is clearly not part of this world. Our soul is clearly divine. We as human beings are clearly the manifestation of The One in human form.

Is condemnation the only way to salvation?

> Thus the Lord, the God of Israel, said to me: 'Take from my hand this cup of wine of wrath, and make all the nations to whom I send you drink it. They shall drink and stagger and be crazed because of the sword which I am sending among them.' (Jeremiah 25: 15, 16).

We are told that Christ died on the cross because He took upon Himself the judgement which had been decided for all mankind. The cup of wrath which was meant for man, Christ drank it in man's place. Thus the cup of wrath became the cup of forgiveness.

Since man was born a sinner according to the Bible as we know it, he, in his natural state, incurs the wrath of God. This sets the scene for a compelling sequence of events. First we have man's sin, then God's wrath directed towards sinful man, then God's wrath followed closely by His judgement. The steps of sin – wrath – judgement form the basis for forgiveness. There is no forgiveness possible otherwise. One has to be guilty and found guilty first so that one can be forgiven. We must accept the idea of the wrath of God and the condemnation of man so that we can believe in the salvation through Christ. In other words, we must accept the wrath of God so that we have the opportunity to experience His Love. No wrath, no love.

As if the existence of love depended on the existence of wrath! As if the qualities of love could not be experienced, defined and understood unless they were contrasted with their direct opposites! As if love were not grounded within itself!

It is sad to see that God has become entangled in our way of thinking.

It is not the God any more whom we acknowledged to be beyond human understanding, so completely different from man and his human nature, so divine. It is another God now, the kind of God who is small enough and human enough to fit into our thinking. Now at last He is our God.

Fortunately for us, God shrugs off our attempts to make Him play the leading role in this sinister game which is played in all earnest by so many people who revel in it. God is far above that. God is the God of Unconditional Love.

Bonsai and free-growing can both be ideal

When looking at a tree which is grown as a bonsai, one may have the impression that it is merely a suggestion of the real tree. Yet, another person may be completely captivated by the bonsai tree, admiring its delicate form, considering it to be a picture of perfection.

In its natural habitat a tree would have the opportunity to respond to its innate desires. And what are they? These desires are the powerful urge to fulfil itself. In the complexity of the urge there are forces at work which complement each other, which strengthen each other, which counteract each other, so that the result is perfect balance, perfect harmony.

This harmony must not be considered a state of being, but a state of becoming, a succession of temporary stages of constant development. The word 'transition' comes to mind because its original meaning is 'going beyond'. A never-ending process of fulfilment which never finds its measure.

A tree which is growing as it was meant to be and where it was meant to be is shaped by its own nature and by the nature of its surroundings. As a result, it is endeavouring to grow according to the plan of its Creator.

The bonsai tree, on the other hand, is to a large degree the expression of the will of a person. Of course, man does not create it, but man controls it. This means that man executes a delicate balancing act: he goes along with the nature of the tree sufficiently to allow it to flourish – to flourish under his control. He prunes the roots, he trims back the branches, he trains the trunk and the branches as he sees fit. And, above all, he provides and controls the soil 'his' tree grows in. Naturally, the tree undergoes constant changes – the changes needed to be alive and to stay alive. They are controlled changes, controlled by an outsider; by the tree's 'contemporary'. They are therefore a far cry from the changes which, under natural conditions, mean development and fulfilment at the same time. The conditions which govern the existence of a bonsai tree do not lead in the direction of its full potential. The bonsai tree is simply marking time.

What has been said can be transposed to a spiritual plane. The free-growing tree can be likened to a person who enjoys the opportunity to make his spiritual journey under a guidance which lies beyond his human understanding. His faith, which is his awareness of the Presence of The One and the certainty of the Unconditional Love of The One are given to him as a precious gift.

The metaphor of a bonsai tree points to a person who is able to lead a spiritually happy and fulfilling life as a member of a church. He does not feel that the organisation of his chosen church, or its religious doctrine, narrows the space which his faith requires. For him his spiritual existence is well-ordered, devoid of insecurity, and – being a faithful member of his church – he is assured of eternal life.

It is for our own personal benefit to be aware of these two different types of spiritual existence. Within ourselves we are free to choose according to our needs and our inclinations. It does not matter what other people think of our choice because it cannot be said that one alternative in itself is better than the other. Each one of us has the God-given right and the freedom to live the spiritual life which is appropriate for this lifetime.

The nature of a promise

When someone makes a promise regarding what he will do or how he will react, he commits himself to something which lies in the future. While it may be argued that the future is simply an extension of the present, we are in no position to say precisely what the future will be like.

The person concerned may change in a direction which cannot be anticipated at the moment of promising. It may even be a change or a development which represents a complete break with the past. Thus what appears to be well within the capabilities of the person at the moment of promising may show itself to be entirely inconceivable in the future. Similarly, the present circumstances may give no indication or may even give misleading indications as to what the situation will be like in the time to come.

After considering these personal imponderables and the circumstantial uncertainties, we must conclude the following: a promise cannot be considered to be a binding commitment. It can only be a statement of intent to do everything possible to meet the obligations agreed on.

In our general way of thinking the idea of a promise is closely associated with the concepts of reliability, responsibility and accountability. In short, a promise is tied in with ethical standards. The first reaction to a broken promise is normally some sort of judgement. Either the person disappointed himself, or he disappointed himself and someone else. And this someone else may hold him responsible whether the promise could be kept or not.

So far all this is simply an aspect of human relationships. However, what is the situation if God becomes involved? What if a promise is made before Him or to Him? Even that would not change the nature of a promise. We may ask, however, whether a broken promise in this case is a sin against God. This point may be an issue with us, but it is certainly not one with God, whose Unconditional Love does not perceive the limitations of human nature as sin.

Let us consider the situation in which no effort has been made to keep a promise even though the circumstances would have been favourable. One might like to say that in this case the lack of effort and intent would be sinful in the eyes of man, but God in His Unconditional Love would look at it differently. Man has a precise knowledge of sinfulness and righteousness, but God has other ideas.

Are we related to our Father?

We call God our Father and we consider ourselves to be His children. Yet, we hesitate to say that God is within us. We lack the courage to say that we are a manifestation of God. It is so obvious that God chose to adopt human form. His Divine Self at our level is our soul. His Divine Self took up temporary residence in our body. We are the manifestation of God in human form.

Heavenly fragrance – a modern parable

Once there was the heavenly fragrance of a heavenly flower. Of course, it had to be made available to all the people so that they could enjoy it, so that it could become part of their daily lives and so that they had access to it all the time.

It was decided that the best way to achieve this was to put it into soap.

That was the easiest way to capture an elusive fragrance. That was the best way to retain it for ever, and that was the best way to dispense it. And, above all, cleanliness is next to godliness.

An industry was set up, people found work in these commercial enterprises and these enterprises in turn needed the support of many other working people. All this, so it was believed, was primarily for the personal benefit of everyone. And it certainly has been for the personal benefit of those who are happy to experience the beautiful fragrance while they are using the soap to make themselves clean.

However, there were others who were not content; who felt that there must be a way to enjoy the beautiful fragrance by itself, not coming from a cake of soap, not associated with the use of water, not accompanied by a good lather. The mere thought of an alternative possibility made them receptive to the gentle moves of the heavenly fragrance to reach people individually. Or was it the other way around? Did the approach of the heavenly fragrance make these people receptive and thus strengthened their desire to enjoy this wondrous gift coming directly from the source?

And now the interpretation. The heavenly fragrance is The One. The transfer of the heavenly fragrance into soap – mixing the Divine with the worldly medium – establishes the God in Three Persons, the functional God. The soap stands for religious doctrine and the industry represents the various churches. Then there are the persons who, among all the hustle and bustle, hear the call which goes out to them as individuals: the call to journey towards The One.

It is quite certain that the increasing tendency to have direct access to the spiritual source is not just part of a general trend of 'back to the basics'.

At the bottom of this strong desire there is the awareness of an even stronger need. Not that the combination of desire and need becomes an unpleasant and irritating urge; not at all. It does become, however, the joyful awareness that a major purpose of one's life has crystallised: direct access to the Spirit.

The Spirit is the breath of life for all of us, no matter how we prefer to be aware of the Spirit, no matter where we prefer to be aware of the Spirit, even no matter whether we are aware of the Spirit at all. The Spirit is totally unavoidable. The Spirit seeks out each and every human being. The Spirit graces each and every human being. The Spirit fills each and every human being in accordance with the capacity of this human being.

By their fire shalt thou know them

Filled with the fire of their faith, they are intent on setting the whole world ablaze. Yet, they are ignorant of the fact that their fire is not the fire of the Burning Bush which burned without destroying. Their fire is kindled and sustained by humans who believe that they are doing the Lord's work in His place.

Is faith without works dead?

So faith by itself, if it has no works, is dead. (James 2: 17).

At first glance this Bible quotation sounds solid, indisputable and absolutely clear. It has the air of a very important directive to the faithful, such is the ring of its authority. However, it is fundamentally flawed within itself.

One must have a thorough look at the key word before embarking on any deliberations. In our case the meaning of the word 'faith' can be given as 'a person's relationship with The One which is essentially an awareness of the Unconditional Love coming from The One'. Our awareness of The One is purely a spiritual experience, a state of consciousness which is outside the realms of time and place.

Within the limitations of our human thinking and the ability to express our thoughts, we can make the following statements about the spiritual relationship between an individual and The One:

There are two poles, so to speak: the individual and The One, or – more precisely – the individual's soul and The One.

The relationship flows between and around the two poles. It flows as energy, it pulsates, it is vibration.

There is no purpose envisaged, or even possible, which lies outside this field of energy.

This field of energy does not depend in the slightest on anything past, present, or yet to come.

Because The One has no beginning and no end, the relationship between The One and the soul also has no beginning and no end.

The reason for the uniqueness of the relationship of The One and the soul is at once surprisingly elementary and totally beyond our comprehension: our soul is divine and as such is part of The One.

Some detail must be given here about the concept of The One. It is very different from the concept of God the Father, God the Son and God the Holy Ghost. Some people may have seen a play which featured several characters, yet there was only one actor as the astonished audience found out at the end of the performance. All the parts were played by just the one actor.

The situation involving the God in Three Persons is structured in a similar way. The roles of God the Father, God the Son and God the Holy Ghost are played out, as it were, by the same Spirit. This one and only Spirit is The One. And The One manifests as God the Father, God the Son And God the Holy Ghost.(1) At this point attention must be drawn to the principle that a manifestation is always different from whatever manifests itself.(2)

Now we have to enlarge on the idea that The One is pure energy; the Universal Life Energy. We know that energy is vibration. We also know that vibration can have varying frequencies. Within our limitations we conclude that the Universal Life Energy firstly is not tied to time and place and, secondly, has a potentially infinite range of frequencies.

Each person's soul is part of The One in a frequency of spiritual energy which is compatible with the mind/body of the person.(3) Furthermore, the soul of a person can, during the person's journey through life, raise its frequency. This is because the spiritual progress during this journey is reflected in corresponding increases in the vibrational frequency of the soul.

The statement that our soul is part of The One may immediately provoke an intense and fervent flurry of thoughts. The usual kind of thoughts. In other words, we are again irresistibly provoked to direct our human thoughts and our human words towards a goal which lies beyond the horizon of our human perception. It is significant that this approach has been practised for many, many generations and it has always failed. It has always failed because it can never succeed.

In conclusion, one may say that it has been absolutely imperative to stand well back and do this extensive groundwork in order to respond appropriately to the topic of this chapter. By faith we understand the spiritual relationship of a person's soul with The One. As such, faith is a self-fulfilling purpose: it is faith for faith's sake. For these reasons the statement that 'by itself, if it has no works, faith is dead' is not a valid proposition.(4)

(1)   The common denominator in these three elements of the God in Three Persons is God. It had to be God because in those days God was considered the ultimate God, the one and only God. Therefore Christ says to God: 'I have manifested thy name to the men . . .' (John 17: 6). If Christ lived today He would speak to The One and say that He has manifested the name of this very One.

(2)   Two well-known manifestations of The One come to mind. On Mount Horeb The One appeared to Moses out of a burning bush which was not consumed by its own fire. (Exodus 3: 4-6). Then, after John had baptised Jesus in the River Jordan and while Jesus was praying, The One appeared as a dove coming from heaven and a voice said: 'Thou art my beloved Son; with thee I am well pleased.' (Luke 3:22). Needless to say that The One is neither a voice, nor a dove, nor a burning bush.

(3)   The situation is reminiscent of the fact that the human body needs and uses a measurable amount of electricity to function. Yet, a much larger and incompatible amount of electricity destroys the person. Similar circumstances exist on the spiritual level. While the Divine Energy at a compatible frequency is the life-giving force for the human being, anything considerably above that level would consume the person. To sum up, we can say that our soul is part of The One, but it is not identical with The One because of the different vibrational frequency levels.

(4)   The topic that faith without works is dead was briefly touched on towards the end of the chapter 'When the Lord makes an approach'. At that time it was said that the statement was correct, with certain provisos. At that time the thoughts expressed were appropriate and valid. Now – quite some time later – that the topic has been considered with greater insight, the result of these recent deliberations is the exact opposite. This complete about-turn may suitably illustrate the fact that while one is making one's journey through life, one is at any given moment at the appropriate point on the path. However, that particular point can never be a final destination, but always is a new point of departure.

Further comment about our faith

What has been said in the preceding chapter implies the principle that there is no need – in fact that there is no room – for a mediator between man's soul and The One.

This relationship between man and The One exists from the very beginning, but man cannot immediately become aware of it. He has to progress a certain distance along the path of his spiritual journey before this awareness can begin to develop. Until this point is reached the individual seems to depend on assistance from his fellow-man to bridge the gap, as it were. The necessary help may come from just one person, or from a group of people, such as a church.

However, once someone is becoming aware of the directness of his relationship with The One, the situation concerning his helpers changes dramatically. What once was necessary help gratefully received now becomes totally unwelcome, a hindrance, even an intrusion.

Why Christ's life as a ransom?

For the Son of man also came . . . to give his life as a ransom for many. (Mark 10:45).

In His teaching Christ had to tune into the prevailing circumstances. He had to work within the framework of the way of life of the people around Him. One of the prevailing ideas was that what was lost had to be redeemed at a price: a ransom had to be paid. A ransom had to be paid even by the Son of God, which means, in fact, even by God Himself.

The question is: 'Who demanded the ransom, to whom was it to be paid, who had to be satisfied by Christ's death?'

Christ said Himself that He was going to fulfil the Will of His Father by sacrificing Himself. Did God demand His Own Son's sacrifice so that He, God, could grant forgiveness of sins to every human being who believed in Christ? Did God actually have to sacrifice part of Himself? And all this as a concession to the way of thinking of the people of those days? Yes, so it seems. All this to make it appear to the people that their redemption was made the right way – their way. 'Indeed, under the law almost everything is purified with blood, and without the shedding of blood there is no forgiveness of sins' – so we read in Hebrews 9, verse 22.

We may find it difficult to look through these events to find the motive

132

behind them. It appears that God had to make so many delaying and irrelevant moves because He could not come out directly with His Unconditional Love. For the people of those days it would have been unthinkable to hear of a Divine Love which was offered without conditions. And yet, all these diversionary steps were obviously motivated by this very Unconditional Love. Because God could not grant it directly He disguised it in Christ's sacrifice. And this makes Christ's death the supreme act of God's Unconditional Love.

In some respects Christ's sacrifice became acceptable to man because a condition was linked with it which allowed man to become a partner in his quest for his salvation. The condition was that he believes in Christ. His belief in Christ who is God the Son was necessary so that God the Father could 'feel free' to forgive him all his sins. These arrangements make Christ's death the ultimate gesture of God to the kind of human being who has to redeem himself in his own eyes, who has to make himself acceptable to God for his own peace of mind.

And the rest of mankind? It is quite simple: all human beings are granted forgiveness of sins in the form of God's Unconditional Love as a matter of principle. Some of them accept it so happily and so gratefully like children when they are offered wondrous gifts. The rest of them perhaps receive it without even realising what is happening to them. Yes, it is a fact, God loves us all, each and every one of us, with His Unconditional Love. And this Unconditional Love seeks out each human being in the special way which is suitable for each particular person.

Our soul is a manifestation to us

Even a moment's reflection would forcefully bring to mind that the soul is a very complex topic. Fortunately, for our purpose only some fundamental observations are required.

The starting premise would be that our soul is immortal since it survives the physical death of its bearer. Since it is immortal it must be divine in its origin and substance. These qualities we can perceive without investigation and reflection because they are self-evident. It is important to be aware of this and to state it clearly because the absence of investigation and reflection creates the quality of total objectivity. Not in all instances can statements be made about spiritual concepts without the involvement of investigation and reflection. Because of its divine nature the soul is completely removed – in its essence – from the range of our mental endeavours. This does not mean, however, that we cannot, must not and should not reflect on it.

Before we embark on any further consideration of the nature of our soul, we must be conscious of the fact that any findings concerning the soul – any statements we are able to formulate in our mind and express in our words – merely refer to and represent a manifestation of the soul. In other words, our findings only create the picture of the soul as we are able to see it with our inner eye. This picture, these thoughts, are bound to be and will always remain a manifestation of the soul. They will never be definitive findings about the soul as such, the soul in its essence.

The revelation of the soul is a gracious act of The One who bends down to our human level of perception, understanding and communication to allow us to satisfy our desire and our need to deal with this divine subject. To put it plainly, the concept of the soul is made accessible to us on our terms; it is made suitable for our human methods of investigation. As much as the quality and the methods of human investigation can vary, so can the concept of the soul vary from person to person.

The One anticipates our thoughts, our questions and our answers. The One gives us the opportunity to establish a relationship which, out of sheer necessity, is contained entirely within our personal sphere, entirely within the limits of our abilities. We may even turn the picture upside down and say that each person 'creates' his own concept of the soul and ultimately his own concept of The One on the basis of his individual spirituality.

Furthermore, it is safe to say that our concept of the soul and our relationship with The One alter to the same extent as our spirituality alters and evolves. Because we are in a constant state of becoming, our spiritual concepts and our relationship with The One are constantly adjusting so that they remain appropriate. This is quite natural, entirely necessary and definitely possible because our concept of The One is only a manifestation of The One to us. As a result, our relationship with The One as we perceive it is, firstly, limited to a given time. Secondly, it is only a manifestation of our real relationship with the real One.

This brings us to the conclusion that manifestations vary according to the spirituality of the person they are destined for. It is important to note that only the manifestations vary, never that which manifests itself.

What has been said so far does not place us, the human being, in front of a huge blank space where we originally expected to find knowledge and understanding of our soul, of The One and of our soul's relationship with The One.

Let us consider our journey. We do not travel across a huge, empty space towards The One. We do not traverse a vast vacuum which lies between us and The One. In addition to that, we do not travel on a path created by our own ideas which continually materialise just a few steps ahead of each traveller, providing us with a solid road surface, so to speak.

We travel on the Divine Energy which is constantly emanating from The One. May we liken it to a monorail with locomotion provided by electromagnetic induction. May we further adapt this comparison and say that there is no rail, there is only the electricity. The Divine Energy is both at the same time: it is the path and it is the propulsion.

Could we use another comparison saying that each one of us travels as if placed on a beam of sunlight. The beam is the path and the propulsion at the same time. Now comes the important realisation: the beam of sunlight comes from the sun, but it is not the sun as such, it is merely the manifestation of the sun. The same principle applies to our journey on the beam of Divine Energy: the Divine Energy is our path and our propulsion. It comes from The One, but it is not The One as such, it is merely a manifestation of The One.

So far our thoughts have been led through three stages. Firstly, we were made to realise that what we are inclined to consider to be our soul, The One, and the relationship of our soul with The One are 'not the real thing'. They are manifestations of the real soul, the real One and of the real relationship of our real soul with the real One.

Secondly, we were shown that the path of our spiritual journey and the energy which takes us along this path are one and the same: Divine Energy.

Thirdly, we have been told that the Divine Energy which simultaneously is our path and our means of progression is not the real One, but only a manifestation of the real One.

Now let us summarize the main points:

Our real soul, the real One and the real relationship of our real soul with the real One are totally beyond our perception, they are the DIVINE TRUTH.

The manifestation to us of our soul, of The One and of the relationship of our soul with The One - these three manifestations are individually created and shaped for each person. They are THE

135

HUMAN TRUTH FOR EACH INDIVIDUAL HUMAN BEING.

Now we are in a position to find meaning in the Bible passage recorded as John 4:24 which says: 'God is spirit, and those who worship him must worship in spirit and truth.' Let us rephrase this to make it appropriate to our spiritual circumstances: 'The One is Spirit and those who worship The One can now worship in keeping with their individual spirituality and their individual truth.'

How long a lifespan?

A relative of ours was a very complete young lady, intelligent, successful in her career, loved by everyone who knew her and adored by her husband and her family. Only a few hours after having given birth to her first child, a beautiful son, complications set in. The skill and dedication of the hospital staff could not save her.

To her relatives and friends her passing was a dreadful shock and a terrible loss. Such a promising young life so cruelly cut short. It just did not make sense.

A day after her transition she appeared to me in broad daylight. I saw her in my mind just clearly enough to realise who she was. After having talked about various matters, she said that she felt very well, very peaceful, and that she would be near us till the day after the funeral. A little later she assured me that she had had a full life and a complete life, that everything would work out fine for her husband and their son.

Two days later she appeared to me once more, telling me again that she had to leave us because her time had come. She said that when the appointed time for a person has come a situation will be created which allows the soul to leave this world.

Then she compared a human life with a book. There are books with many pages and there are books with a relatively low number of pages, but the number of pages does not matter. The story contained in a thin book can still be very happy, full of meaning and perfectly complete in itself. And so was her life.

It is only natural that, when a person dear to us leaves us, we feel that this loved one has been taken away from us. If this person did not live at least three score years and ten, as mentioned in the Bible as we know it, a strong feeling of disappointment - even injustice - combines with our deep sense of loss. Certainly, sadness must be experienced and this sadness must be expressed. However, the healing of the wound must follow. The adequate time of mourning our loved one's death must give way to celebrating our loved one's life.

Jesus, God and the Holy Ghost – or The One?

In line with the realisation that Jesus, God and the Holy Ghost are manifestations of The One, the way we refer to them has to be looked at.

There do not appear to be any problems associated with the term 'Jesus' because He was a person of flesh and blood. It is therefore quite in order to refer to Him with words such as 'He, Him, Himself' which give Him human features in addition to His spiritual qualities.

The situation concerning the word 'God' is quite different. In the Bible as we know it God plays the role of the highest instance: He is the supreme ruler in the spiritual realm. This role of God certainly met the requirements of the people of the biblical days and subsequent centuries. It equally still meets the requirements of the people of our time who accept this role as the ultimate belief for themselves. For those who have travelled further spiritually during their life's journey the concept of God as He appears in the Bible is not acceptable as their truth, as the ultimate formulation of their belief. For them God cannot be treated as a male person, cannot love and hate like a human being, cannot – in essence – be described with human words and cannot be understood with human thoughts. To put it differently, it is imperative for these people to find a new way to refer to their highest spiritual being.

The term 'The One' has been the breakthrough. 'One' is a well-known word which has been elevated to a title with a very specific meaning, conveying a unique notion. The One is the source of all spiritual manifestations, including Jesus, God and the Holy Ghost.(1) The One can be referred to only as The One and even then we must be aware that the three letters 'o, n, e' are human inventions, are part of our human language and cannot capture at all the Essence of The One. We must always be mindful that the term 'The One' is only a symbol, a linguistic symbol, for what is beyond our horizon.

And this is where the linguistic problems begin. Let us look at Genesis 2:2 which reads 'And on the seventh day God finished his work which he had done, and he rested on the seventh day from all his work which he had done.'(2) The words 'he' and 'his' refer to God in the most natural way because God is also the Father. However, 'he' and 'his'

137

cannot be used in reference to The One because The One is not something else as well – like the God who is also the Father – because The One has no human features. In fact, it is to be assumed that The One has no other features at all. What we think are features of The One – part of the Essence of The One – are actually manifestations. For example, we are aware of a Universal Life Force, we are conscious of a Will at work, we acknowledge the existence of the Truth, we feel that we are blessed by Unconditional Love: all these are manifestations of The One.

The situation is quite clear. The limitations of our language force us to continue using the word 'God' when we actually do not wish to express the various meanings which it conveys in the Bible. However, we cannot and do not allow the constraints of our human language to restrict our spiritual experience and development. All we have to do to achieve this is to remain mindful of the double meaning of the word 'God': firstly the God of the Bible, secondly The One.

Now the decisive question arises: will we persist with our efforts to capture the Essence of The One with our language patterns? If we decide to do that we will attempt to bring The One down to our level of understanding as the biblical God was brought down. And this will effectively mean that we will – with great devotion – bestow one human attribute after another on The One. And this in turn will mean that we will create The One in our image. And this will effectively mean that we create an idol – not with our hands as the 'non-believers' do – but with our thoughts and with our words as the 'believers' do.

We must acknowledge and accept that the awareness of the existence of The One cannot be developed into a comprehensive thought structure, a doctrine, as it were. And without a doctrine there is little possibility of creating and maintaining churches as we know them.(3) The One is definitely and entirely beyond us human beings and that is why manifestations of The One like Jesus, God and the Holy Ghost have been and will be in this world for those of us who need them and for whom they are the ultimate truth.

(1) Because the Holy Ghost is not provided with human qualities, because it is not presented as a person, its role is not as defined as the parts played by God the Father and God the Son. It is much more abstract than the other two elements of the Trinity and therefore also much more elusive.

(2) If this passage were to be rewritten, it would begin like this:

'And on the seventh day The One finished The One's work which The One had done.'

(3)   There is, however, the possibility of a new kind of church, the Church of Love envisaged by the Cathar Prophesy of 1244 A.D. which states in part:

'It has no fabric, only understanding.
It has no membership, save those who know they belong.
It has no rivals, because it is non-competitive.
It has no ambition, it seeks only to serve.'
(Fuller, Simon Peter: *Rising Out of Chaos*; p 200)

Is man separated from God?

The further away from man, the more superior to man. The higher above man, the more divine. God and man, shall the twain ever meet?

They did meet once, quite ostentatiously so, according to the Bible as we know it: there came Christ. The son of man and the Son of God, man and God in the same person. He was not welcome to the spiritual establishment because He did not fit the established pattern. The traditional thinking could not deal with such a phenomenon. Yet, to deal with this situation it had. The only way left on the spiritual level was to reject it, to attack it. Yet, in real life, in the existing world, in every person, in every human being, there have always been God and man: the divine soul in a human body. There has always been this linkage between God and man. Its reality is totally independent of whether it is noticed, whether it is understood, whether it is accepted. The human mind is not a factor in the creation of the physical and the spiritual circumstances of our human existence. Simply because the human mind is also a product of this creation. Sadly, though, in many instances the human mind creates its own world by equating its perception of the world with the actual and factual nature of the world.

The combination of the human and the Divine is, to many people's thinking, absurd. It is unacceptable to their logic. It does not make sense. It cannot be imagined and the conclusion is that it cannot exist.

This intellectual conclusion seems to be confirmed and further strengthened by practical observation. There is no doubt that human behaviour, viewed individually or collectively, quite often does not give an indication of the dual nature of man. Quite often it is utterly devoid of divine inspiration, quite often it almost forces the observer to wonder whether there is indeed such a phenomenon as divine inspiration, even whether the Divine exists at all.

What has been said so far presents some of the reasons why man is perceived to be in a state of separation from the Divine. This state of separation is not only the impression which the outside observer may arrive at. It may also be the feeling which the individual has of his own state of being.

'Don't let surface things delude us' it says in the Aramaic Lord's Prayer. On the surface we are dealing with opposites, mainly with good and bad. Good is readily associated with the Divine and bad stands for human. To suggest that the human being is potentially either good or bad at every single moment of his lifetime here on earth would be acceptable to our logical thinking. However, to suggest that the human being is both good and bad at every moment of his existence here on earth is not logical. The notion that there is a fusion of good and bad is absurd. And yet, it is a reality, a reality which resists attempts to define it in simple terms. It manifests itself in two steps, as it were. Firstly, it abolishes the concept of good and bad. Secondly, it fails to replace these two concepts with a single notion of logical nature. We are left with a void which, so it seems, can be filled only with something transcendental. Furthermore, it appears that as soon as an attempt to pull this transcendental value into our human sphere of perceptions is made it vanishes like a snowflake in our hand. An attempt to put one of our human notions in place – such as 'the truth', or 'God's Will' – offers most likely only a short-lived solution. A solution which immediately opens up a new area of inquiries, of calls for clarification, of efforts to grasp what lies beyond us.

The idea of man's oneness with God may not be generally accepted. Man's oneness with God may not be a decisive factor in each individual's life here on earth. It may be difficult to explain. Some of us may not have noticed even a trace of it. For others it may already be an awareness, perhaps only the beginning of an awareness. For others it may have had the opportunity to grow into a powerful force. A person's perception of his oneness with God is not the final result of a development which would mean the end of this development. There can only be a constantly growing awareness of God, a constant movement towards God. Man's oneness with God is always in the making. Sooner or later the moment will come when the person is inspired to say: 'I feel at one with the Divine in my soul. It is all a mystery to me, but I know that it is true.'

The nature of our spiritual awareness

The following thoughts on the nature of our spiritual awareness were part of a conversation with my guide 16th July 1994. They were put forward by my guide and were recorded word for word.

. . . to come back to that word 'awareness'. I know you like it; you've always been keen to balance that cold-blooded mind-thinking with the brain with – what you like to call – 'thinking with the heart'. And awareness is actually thinking with the heart.

This is the gateway for metaphysical growth. It is the door from our, or your, human limitations which manifest themselves in the limitations of brain-thinking. Well, awareness starts off really strongly where brain-thinking peters out. Yep, there are no limitations to awareness because awareness is a function of the soul. The Germans have a good word for the main characteristics of awareness: it is the word 'Ahnung'.(1) No limitations to awareness because the soul constantly raises its vibrations as a result of its increasing awareness.(2) One nourishes the other, one raises the other. Yes, you are quite right, like a perpetuum mobile. No point in looking for another one because that is the only one around.(3)

Manifestation of the Spirit. Can even say that the manifestation of the Spirit is Spirit.(4) Remember that introduction to philosophy? When you read that in the Divine all differences cease to exist, all contrasts: where a = non-a? And you grasped that, not bad. See, that was awareness, it was not understanding.

. . . Well, I am inclined to say: 'And here endeth the lesson.'

In conclusion we can say that the awareness of our spirituality is synonymous with the awareness of The One's Presence within us, of The One's Unconditional Love filling us. And the further we travel along the path of our spiritual journey, the greater our capacity to receive this Unconditional Love.

(1) In this context the meaning of the word 'Ahnung' may be described as a combination of indefinable feeling, intuitive knowing and gentle hoping.
(2) In other words, the increasing spiritual awareness of the soul raises the soul's vibrations. Higher vibrations in turn increase the spiritual awareness. This is potentially a never-ending process.
(3) To mean that this is the only perpetuum mobile which is and ever will be.

(4) Normally the manifestation is always different from what manifests itself. However, when the manifesting takes place within the Divine, this principle does not apply. Let us consider the following:

For Spirit we put: a
For manifestation we put: non-a
In the Divine all differences
are dissolved, therefore: $a = \text{non-}a$

This is a wonderfully uncomplicated illustration of the principle that at the divine level all is one, there is only The One.

Life on earth: a climb or a journey?

It has been a long-standing habit of mankind to look up in awe to what is above, above the human being. A gigantic tree, the threatening clouds of a storm, lightning and thunder, a beautiful morning sky, the sun, the stars, the moon and a magnificent rainbow which is said to be the sign of peace – all these above, all these we look up to. The purely physical situation which surrounds us and which dictates to us shows the way for many of our actions and for much of our behaviour. It provides the pattern and, as a result, it shapes our attitude: we do not just look up, but we look up in awe.

When we consider our position among our fellow-men, we realise that there are some beneath us and some above us. As we progress in our jobs and vocations we find that some of us rise to great heights. It does not take long for the aspect of value to become apparent: higher up means more successful, more impressive, more respectable, more inspiring, more advanced – it simply means better. Thus the assessment of one's own position, the positions of others, inevitably leads to judgement. Development, progress and even the persons themselves are judged and the findings are recorded on a vertical scale. Interestingly enough, the word 'scale' is derived from the Latin word 'scala' which in this context means 'ladder, flight of steps'.

However, there is an alternative situation we can put ourselves in. Instead of the traditional up and down movement, up and down the scale of values, there is another possibility: movement on the same level all the time. This movement is best described as a journey, a journey along one's path of life. Along this path each one of us progresses, each one of us advances. We are all on the same level, yet we do not have to be the same. We all retain our individuality, yet we are at the same eye-level, we are equal in each other's eyes.

Our individuality is strictly spiritual as we advance along the path of increasing awareness of the Presence of God in each one of us. Some of the aspects of God's Presence we can actually formulate in our mind, such as His Divine Energy and His Divine Will which we know are constantly at work within us and around us. This process of increasing awareness can be likened to a never-ending awakening. To us the Divine has manifested not as a person, but as a constant Presence, a Divine Energy, a Divine Will, Unconditional Love, the Truth and ultimately as The One.

Along this kind of journey through life there is no frantic striving, there is no competition for top position, there is no need to try so hard, there is no need to assert oneself, there is no desire to outdo one's fellow-man. In addition, we do not have to make ourselves acceptable to God, to make ourselves better than we are in His eyes because He created us as we are. He would certainly not spurn His own handiwork, but He would surely allow humanity to accept and enjoy His Unconditional Love.

Instead of competition with our fellow-men and an attempt to dominate the world around us there is growth, growth within. During this journey the distance covered – if one may use the word 'distance' – is totally irrelevant, entirely meaningless. It is a journey without end. Each moment and each point along the path is an achievement in itself. For this reason the journey does not have to have an end here on earth. There is no need for the glory of reaching a destination, indeed there is no place for such feelings. And why not? Because the journey continues in the life hereafter.

Is it easy to forgive oneself?

Some people have experienced the existence of two types of forgiveness. There is the kind of forgiveness which is related to our faith, a forgiveness which we constantly receive in the Unconditional Love of The One. Believing in The One is generally synonymous with believing in Unconditional Forgiveness and accepting it unconditionally.

It may sound strange that for some of us it is a lot easier to accept the forgiveness coming from The One than to forgive oneself. For some of us it is so simple to let The One, as it were, do the forgiving. In this case I know that I am loved, and I am loved as I am, no matter what I do, no matter what I have done. In spite of these realisations I sometimes feel that it is absolutely necessary that I also forgive myself for what I consider I should not have done.

When I have done something silly, something negative on the spur of the moment, when I should have known better . . . I accuse myself. And I can do that well, at times relentlessly, with my emotions magnifying the factual circumstances. The matter in question need not necessarily be important, something trivial will do most times. And why is that so? 'Because I am a worrier and it has nothing to do with pride' would be the likely answer. Although I know that The One does not judge me, I cannot help 'going into judgement with myself'. I can certainly rationalise the situation, saying that the mistake I made is simply an indication that I am human, even that the mistake could have been intended as a reminder of my human imperfections.

What if my emotions do not listen to my mind? Then I have to go to my faith and build a bridge between the forgiveness granted freely by The One and the forgiveness I have to ask from my self. It may not be easy at times, it may be slow at times.

Call it an affirmation, use it like a prayer, like a mantra – no matter what it is – it was given to me in a time of difficulty. The words are best said three times to increase the effect. They can be used as often as required. They can be said in one' s mind, but saying them out aloud seems to give a better result. The words which came to me in the same way as this whole writing are as follows:

> I can forgive myself
> And I am forgiving myself.
> I love myself as I am
> Because God loves me as I am.

About spiritual communication

There are various forms and ways in which a spirit communicates with a person of flesh and blood and – spirit. These methods have one thing in common, though: they are likely to appear rather incredible to the uninitiated and even to be fraudulent trickery to the self-centered critic. This is quite natural as an emission coming from one point needs to be received at another point in order to become a communication. A person's doubt about such a phenomenon has no bearing whatsoever on the existence of such an emission. Doubt or even denial are simply indications that the person is not able – yet – to receive spiritual communication.

It is not intended to give comprehensive information about spiritual communication. Only certain aspects will be dealt with as they literally come to mind.

We receive impulses more often than we realise. It happens from time to time, for instance, that we move around in town seemingly aimlessly till we 'run into' someone we are happy to meet. Someone we already know or even a stranger. These cases definitely involve spiritual communication, albeit at a subconscious level. In the end we may realise what has been going on and say to ourselves: 'Ah, that's why I have been drifting around.'

Spiritual communication can range from mere impulses to quite detailed messages. A very gentle and low key variation can happen to a person in response to something which happens in his presence. When the witness sees or hears something, he may experience a flow of energy entering his body, perhaps running down his spine, perhaps filling his whole body. At the same time he may glide into a slightly altered state of consciousness. It seems that in most cases this is a way of receiving confirmation of the positive nature of what has happened or the truth of what has been said in the person's presence.

On occasions one may see before one's inner eye the image of a person, of someone who is still living on this earth, or of someone who has already made his transition. The image may be static, like a photograph, or there may be movement, words may be spoken, even a conversation may develop. This may happen without prior notice, without any conscious intent of the recipient, even in broad daylight, slotted, as it were, into the recipient's daily routine.

Similarly, unexpected verbal messages may appear, providing the person with timely reminders, answers to questions which have occupied his mind, or simply assuring him of the caring presence of a loved one.(1)

In a significantly altered state of consciousness several types of spiritual communication may combine. Meditation seems to provide an ideal condition for this to happen. There may be a clear visual presentation complemented by sound, similar to a film. The person may even play a dual role: he himself can be an active member of the cast and at the same time the only spectator. What is also remarkable is the fact that everything is remembered in detail later on, even by persons who normally cannot remember dreams.

While one is asleep one may also receive the full range of spiritual emissions which may take on the nature of a dream.

To experience the presence of a spirit on the abstract, spiritual level is to witness the manifestation of this spirit in the form of an apparition. To experience the presence of a spirit on the concrete, physical level embodied in a person of flesh and blood means to come face to face with an incarnation. The latter happened to me during a Reiki seminar in 1992. I found the presence of one of the ladies to be initiated very special on the spiritual level. During one of the sessions I went into a trance and was told that she was the incarnation of my sister who was stillborn in 1936. This fact was confirmed to me in two separate meditations within the following two or three years.

In these days of ever-increasing spiritual awakening it happens quite often that, when meeting a perfect stranger, one feels that one has known that person before. Did one know the other person in a previous lifetime, or is it simply because now is the time that soul groups are finding each other and are coming together? Whatever it may be, it is a manifestation of spiritual communication, the giving and receiving of compatible spiritual energy.

People who have moved across the line to the other side – be they relatives, friends or strangers – are potential ghosts or potential spiritual guides as far as we are concerned. It depends entirely on our point of view, our spiritual attitude, our whole personality what we make of these visions.

It must be stated that the soul of a person who is still in this life can also be a spiritual guide for other people who are still alive physically, if it has been so decided. In this case spiritual energy is sent to the other person who may receive it consciously or subconsciously. Naturally, the sender of this spiritual energy is not being drained or weakened, since his soul is not the source, since it is not acting on its own behalf, being only a channel. It is merely a part of the whole, of the never-ending flow and circulation of spiritual energy: it receives in order to give.

The 'intense' presence of spiritual energy, be it just as energy or in the manifestation of a spirit, is a powerful experience for the person who is being visited. One can physically be shaken vigorously which seems to reach down to the foundations of one's personality. This condition is a fairly unusual state of being which may differ from case to case. There may be no emotions at all, there is no pain, the physical shaking is not even unpleasant for the person who experiences it while it would be somewhat upsetting for those who are watching it. In this case the visiting spiritual energy is of a much higher vibrational frequency than the vibration of the person who is receiving it. This causes such an unusual reaction. There is no doubt that this kind of exposure permanently raises the recipient's vibrational frequency, helping him along on his spiritual journey.

As the level of collective spirituality has been rising in our time, so has the occurrence of oral and written channelling. There are many audio recordings of such communications and numerous books which were practically dictated. The extent to which the medium is in a trance can vary considerably. In written channelling the profound state of altered consciousness can decrease gradually at the same rate as the medium's vibrational frequency rises. It will then perhaps become a floating sensation of inspiration in which the self plays no part. The source of inspiration, the guide, so to speak, can perhaps be identifiable, frequently even having a name which may be real or fictitious. Knowledge of the identity of the source seems to be important in some cases. In other instances this detail appears to be of no consequence and does not even arouse the slightest ripple of curiosity.

During my early stages of consciously receiving spiritual energy and communication, my guides announced their presence with calling signs. These were pre-arranged spots on the crown of my head, two on the left side and the third one on the right. The signal was a buzzing kind of energy which would turn itself off once the communication got under way. On some occasions these three spots would also double as receiving centres for energy, similar to chakras.

For my writing I had my father-in-law as a guide for some time. He was a Presbyterian minister and was especially helpful with Bible quotations. Unfortunately, I never met him as a person. Fairly early in the piece he said that he wanted to make up for the things he had preached from the pulpit and which he cannot agree with now. At one stage he also told me that his spirit and my spirit would merge and that I would be his spiritual heir. As a result, while I have been writing, the inspiration has been non-personal, just inspiration.

He spoke to me directly only when we conversed about various topics including their concept of teamwork. The guides do not necessarily function side by side, or take turns. Being pure energy, they can super-impose one on the other, as my guide put it, combining their energies. Their separate identities in which they manifest to us are merely concessions to our human understanding. We must also consider that what to us is one entity can divide into parts and these can merge with different entities.

The principle of a compound soul can also apply to a person living here on earth. One may be inclined to think that a person is the reincarnation of one particular soul. This may well be the case. However, this individual soul may be joined by part of another soul, or parts of other souls. Since souls, like the Divine, are pure energy they have no shape. For this reason the possibilities of combinations are absolutely unlimited. Mergers may take place in the spirit world before the reincarnation, or they may happen here on earth after the reincarnation.

A person of flesh and blood may feel indications of whose spiritual entities – if they can be linked to persons – have contributed to the composition of his soul. This information may also come from another person of flesh and blood, a psychic person, as it happened to me once.

May I shed some light on the possible nature of a spiritual guide within the limitations of my understanding. In addition, I would like to say that what I was told may refer to my case only, it may only be 'my truth'. Here is part of a conversation which took place on the 16th of July 1994:

Self: . . . are you helping and guiding me . . .?
Guide: Yes, I am.
Self: Anybody else?
Guide: Yes, the Lord.
Self: How does that work?
Guide: We are the servants of the Lord. He gives us jobs to do. It's not that he says 'do this', or 'do that'. Yes, you are thinking of programming. It's a bit like that, but I'd like to call it implanting. He puts part of His Will into us and from that moment on that Will becomes a self-contained entity and guides us. It is like a person in each one of us. It is actually the Lord in each one of us. It is, one might also say, that each one of us is the body for part of the Lord. In other words, we are the embodiment of the Lord. When I use the

word 'body' I mean a spiritual body. You understand that, don't you? You have for a long time been able to think in contradictions . . .

It may be added here that a 'guide being' has a strong structural similarity with a 'human being'. The human being has a human body and a divine soul. The guide has a spiritual body and a Divine Will. And that is where the similarity ends. The human being is subject to possible conflict between its divine soul and its human body. The spiritual guide can only be in divine harmony with the Divine Will. And here we have reached the limit of our thoughts which satisfy and perhaps even flatter our human nature, but which – in reality – can lead us only to complete capitulation before what is 'beyond understanding'. At this point understanding quite happily gives way to joyful awareness.

In spiritual communication, generally speaking, different languages present no problems. There is normally no language barrier. At first glance it may seem that the guide communicates in the recipient's language or languages. The situation is somewhat different, however. Any spiritual communication is amorphous, consisting of impulses of spiritual energy as it were. When it reaches the recipient the spiritual energy then manifests as words and meanings which are suitable for the recipient.(2)

A few years ago it was demonstrated to me that in spiritual communication – one higher self communicating with another higher self – the recipient hears the message in his language. It happened to me in Peru. It was a very special encounter. I had laboriously said something in broken Spanish. The next moment I went into a trance which lasted just long enough for me to hear the other person's response in the most beautiful English. Yet, the other person could not speak English.

What I have said about some aspects of spiritual communication is based partly on my own experience and partly on that of others. Spiritual communication seems to be of a very individual nature and while all cases appear to have certain characteristics in common, each case can have its own particular features.

(1) Spiritual sources are not necessarily always serious and solemn in spiritual appearance and utterance. While I was receiving the first part of 'Heavenly fragrance – a modern parable' I had the feeling that somebody was having a bit of

149

fun, giving me the words tongue in cheek. 'They' certainly also have a sense of humour. By the way, the interpretation came through almost two years later!

(2) The whole situation reminds us of our telecommunications. Let us look at the pioneer in this area, the telephone. Electrical impulses are sent out from one point and are received at another point. The impulses of physical energy are transformed by a technical device so that they 'manifest' – become noticeable and meaningful – to the person who is listening.

With electronic communication physical energy is transformed by a physical device to become physical communication. In analogy, one might venture to say that spiritual energy sent out to somebody is transformed – manifests – in the spiritual part of that person, in his soul, to become spiritual communication.

Man and God's Unconditional Love

God's assurance to us that He loves us with true love, with Unconditional Love, is absolute. We do not have to consider ourselves as deserving of it, we do not have to change and rise to a specific level where we are deemed worthy of it.

Because God's Unconditional Love is pure Divine Energy, it moves only in one direction, from Him to each one of His children, to each one of us. Being Divine, it is not and it cannot be influenced by anything else. It cannot even be approached by anything else. It is an energy which is constantly at work, which constantly flows to us, fills us and surrounds us. Every single moment of our lives.

This wonderful gift which surpasses all human understanding practically begs us to accept it. Even though it is always in and around us it still seeks our acceptance. Whether we accept it or whether we decline it certainly does not affect it at all. God's Unconditional Love is what it is, what it always was and what it will be for ever.

And how do we respond? From our general point of view, because of the limitations of our human nature, we may consider this incomprehensible gift so overwhelming that it can be a mixed blessing for some of us. It can be so awe-inspiring, so over-powering that we cannot bear it. If we feel that way we must realise that we are trying to understand it. Trying to understand it in actual fact means trying to dominate it with our mind. This is so because the ultimate purpose of developing an understanding of something is not the gaining of knowledge because the process does not stop there. It goes a step further since we use knowledge to secure our position in this world of ours. Knowledge is our means of dominating, of surviving by dominating, of being superior, of being in control. Knowledge is power. Trying to understand God's Unconditional Love in effect means trying to be above it on the intellectual level. Since this is not possible, those of us who have no alternative approach have to conclude that the concept of God's Unconditional Love is illogical, absurd and therefore totally unacceptable.

In the Bible as we know it we seem to find a solution to this dilemma. It is so simple because it is a concession to the limitations of our human nature. The magic formula is: 'Believe in God and He loves you.' As a result, we do not have to accept this almost unbelievable gift from God passively, just holding out our hands in gratitude and wonderment. No, we do something to make ourselves worthy of it and being worthy of it we are entitled to it. Effectively, we receive from God only what He owes us according to the arrangement between us and Him. Everything is perfectly sound and logical. The situation is under control. We are in control.

Is this really a solution? Of course not. Since the love we are promised if we believe is merely a reward, the arrangement with God destroys the meaning of the word 'love'. It also destroys the divine nature of the gift from God. Furthermore, it ultimately puts up a barrier between us and God. Not an insurmountable obstacle for God, naturally, but one which makes it so much harder for us to become more and more aware of His Presence which we generally perceive as His Unconditional Love.

The Holy Ghost

The Holy Ghost appears in the New Testament under various names, such as 'the Spirit of God' (Matthew 3:16), as 'the Spirit' (Mark 1:10,11; John 1:32) and as 'the Holy Spirit' (Luke 3:22; John 1:33).

In some instances the Holy Ghost acts independently, descending on the disciples on the day of Pentecost (Acts 2:1-4), to mention only one example. Then again the Holy Ghost is bestowed by Jesus as foreshadowed by John the Baptist with the words '. . . this is he who baptises with the Holy Spirit'. (John 1: 33).

Of course, it is not possible to distinguish clearly between God, Jesus and the Holy Ghost within the concept of the Trinity. Whether we consider all three of them as manifestations of The One or as ultimate spiritual truths in their own right makes no appreciable difference. We can be aware of the Trinity to varying degrees, but we cannot understand it to a point where we can accommodate it in our mind as 'controllable' knowledge.

One thing appears to be quite clear: the manifestations of The One as God and as Jesus are greater concessions to our desire for understanding than the manifestation which is known as the Holy Ghost. It could even be said that the Holy Ghost as a more abstract and therefore a more elusive manifestation may be considered to be the forerunner of the concept of The One. However, the Holy Ghost has been no more than a pointer. It can be no more than that because it is tied in with the other two parts of the Trinity, the manifestations of God the Father and God the Son. We have to realise that The One is not at all accessible to our thoughts, that The One appears to us only as a Presence, as an indefinable Presence.

All of us, either as individuals or as groups, are always free to draw our own conclusions concerning the thoughts expressed in this writing. This chapter may be a strong case in point.

Has the Bible been translated correctly?

The topic of this chapter is identical with the title of two volumes written by Pinchas Lapide, Professor of Jewish theology who held, among other academic positions, a prominent post at the Bar-Ilan-University in Israel. These two books represent only a fraction of Pinchas Lapide's scientific writing. As they are critical studies of Bible translations into German, they had to be written in German. And, because they concern specifically Hebrew and German, they cannot be translated into other languages, it appears.

Pinchas Lapide calls for a critical appraisal of the Bible translations into German and suggests essential corrections.(1) One might think that this implies that Bible translations into other languages should also be looked at.

It must be realised that translating a piece of writing is not a simple matter. There is more to it than taking one word at a time from the

152

original text, replacing it with the equivalent word of the target language and then adapting and arranging these newly obtained words according to the internal structure of the target language. Translating is such a complex skill that it must be called an art. At the same time it is a fastidious science, taking in a vast range of knowledge outside the area of linguistics. A translator of biblical texts worth his salt and honest with himself is aware of his difficulties or even his inability to transform the original into another language. There are shades of meaning, levels of speech, connotations, cultural content which are all to be transposed into the target language which is the language of a people with a very different culture and who live in a very different age.

It is not possible to translate without interpreting in the sense that the translator has to decide which words to choose from a number of possibilities. Sometimes none of the possibilities can be considered to be satisfactory, yet it is impossible to leave a gap. The German reformer Martin Luther (1483-1546) who translated the Bible into German was clearly aware of his agonising role as a translator.(2)

Once a text has been produced in the target language, that is not the end of the matter. Far from it, it is only the beginning. Because the translation is now elevated to the rank of an original text, it is the starting point of a variety of activities. These range from the simple reading by an individual to providing the basis for learned research, for discussion and further development of ideas. And in turn, this new-found knowledge is tinged with the understanding and interpretation of its contributors.

Now let us look at some physical aspects of the production of the Bible. The first translation of the Hebrew Bible, the Greek Septuaginta, was completed about 300 years before Christ's birth. It was written by hand, naturally, and had to be copied by hand. Until the use of the printing press after about 1460 copies of the Bible, be they in Greek or in Latin, had to be written by hand. In the Middle Ages this work was usually done by monks in a room set aside for this purpose in their monasteries where it was common practice that the text was dictated to a number of copyists. There was a long succession of copies being copied. The number of variations in these handwritten texts must have been considerable. First there were the shortcomings of the initial translations. Then there were the inaccuracies caused by the copying. Not only was the Old Testament affected, but also the Greek text of the New Testament.(3)

The interpretation of entire passages can also lead to distortions. In an effort to prove that Jesus was indeed the expected Messiah, some writers of the New Testament used passages from the Old Testament, interpreted them and endowed them with prophetic qualities.

One such passage is Isaiah 7: 14 where we read: 'Therefore the Lord himself will give you a sign. Behold, a young woman shall conceive and bear a son, and shall call his name Immanuel.' And, furthermore, Isaiah says to his King Ahaz that '. . . before the child knows how to refuse the evil and choose the good, the land before whose two kings you are in dread will be deserted.' (verse 16). So promised Isaiah his King Ahaz in this historically documented situation about 730 years before Jesus was born. This picture in words was meant to show Ahaz that God's help was present, Immanuel meaning 'God with us'. It is very difficult to see any connection between this historic episode and the birth of Christ.

Yet, in Matthew we hear of an angel of the Lord speaking to Joseph about Mary, saying: 'She will bear a son, and you shall call his name Jesus, for he will save his people from their sins.' (1: 21). Then Matthew tells us that all this took place to fulfil what the Lord had spoken by the prophet, adding: 'Behold a virgin shall conceive and bear a son, and his name shall be called Emmanuel' (which means, God with us). (1: 23).

There are discrepancies in this short passage written by Matthew. Isaiah speaks of a young woman, whereas Matthew uses the word 'virgin'. Isaiah, when speaking to King Ahaz, says that the expected boy will be called Immanuel. This is correctly quoted by Matthew, but it contradicts the words spoken by the angel which instruct Joseph to call Mary's son Jesus.(4)

There are also serious misunderstandings abroad of the true nature of the Five Books of Moses. They are mainly due to the incorrect translation of the Hebrew name 'Torah' into 'The Law'.

Pinchas Lapide points out that in the Torah there is written more about good news, promise, realised expectations, stories of salvation and ethos than 'laws', statutes and directions which are all meant to further human ethos and social justice. More than two thirds of the Hebrew Bible have nothing to do with legality, but are dedicated to the acts of love which God granted His people Israel. The instructions set out in the Torah are complied with voluntarily because they instil love and call for a higher level of human development. Love and commandment do not stand opposite each other as a contrast, but represent a harmony. To translate the word 'Torah' with the words 'The Law' is totally wrong linguistically and with regard to the contents of the writing called 'Torah'.(5)

Already the very first book of the Bible presented difficulties for the translators. The English, French and German Bibles used in connection with 'God, You and Love' all show the same translation of the original Hebrew text of Genesis 1: 28. And their version is tragically different from the source. This translation states that God said to man: 'Be fruitful and multiply, and fill the earth and subdue it; and have dominion . . . over every living thing that moves upon the earth.' In the Hebrew original man is commanded 'to take care of God's world, not to subdue it; to reign, not to usurp; to administer in a wise and circumspect manner, to preserve and to develop as a steward of God, who has entrusted this good creation to his children.'(6)

Again we are made aware – perhaps painfully aware – of the fact that all our endeavours are 'of this world'. Our deliberations concerning the Bible as we know it should actually begin on premises which are outside our knowledge, such as the cultural and language situation in which the ancient Hebrews and then, later on, Christ lived.

Having missed this prerequisite, we move on regardless to the writing handed down to us by the various translators who did their humanly best to convert into our language and our way of thinking what in many cases is unique and has no equivalent in any other language. Quite clearly, the text they provide can only be an approximation – but we take it for gospel. We attribute to it the status of absolute and eternal validity.

Then we continue our efforts, attempting to achieve the impossible: we try to reconcile or eliminate the differences and contradictions which have been handed down to us. To this end we engage all the power of our human mind. The inescapable end result is not a final result, it is only a further approximation.

However, we cannot be deterred, we continue the absurd effort, the crowning effort: to capture in thought and in word the Essence of The One whom we acknowledge to be 'beyond understanding'.

(1)   Lapide, Pinchas: *Has the Bible been translated correctly?* Vol. 1, p 60 ff
(2)   ibid. vol 1, p 19 ff: 'Luther's Struggle with the Scriptures'
(3)   ibid. vol 1, p 28
(4)   ibid. vol 1, p 29, 30
(5)   ibid. vol 1, p 43 ff

The reader is reminded that the chapters 'The Old Testament and the New Testament today' and 'Man is justified by his faith and not by his works' contain some superseded information.

(6)   ibid. vol 1, p 62

Incorrect Bible translations and 'God, You and Love'

It is important that we assess the implications which incorrect Bible translations may have for this writing.

First we have to clarify what today's Bible is for us. For us it has two major aspects: it consists of translations into our language and it is a work of literature in its own right. Whether the translations are accurate renderings of the originals is – in the practical sense – a problem which is beyond the average person who reads the Bible as we know it or who is instructed according to the Bible as we know it.

This writing has made use of the Bible in certain ways. At times it used Bible passages as starting points and, in other instances, it obtained material from the Bible for the development of its own ideas. Some of these ideas are compatible with what the Bible says whereas others move in a different direction. From this angle, this writing is very much like any expression of spiritual ideas which has been put forward ever since the Bible in its present form has existed.

At the same time this writing has a character of its own. It is a record of the writer's spiritual development. Not so much a description of his spiritual journey, but it is the progressive presentation of the spiritual elements which initiated and sustained particular stages of development. It is quite clear, however, that this writing was conveyed for its own sake, even though it was addressed to an individual to become part of his life. The significance of this writing for the person who recorded it is enormous and firmly established. Its significance for anybody else depends completely on the reader: through his reactions he creates its importance or its unimportance for himself.

May it be stated again that this writing does not present itself with an air of authority because it does not claim general validity. In fact, it does not lay claim to anything. Its purpose is just to be there.

It certainly has put forward ideas and concepts. It certainly has presented these sometimes as valid, meaning valid within its own perimeter. Sometimes reference has been made to ideas and concepts which were found to be invalid – invalid within its own perimeter. And that was all.

It was not intended that what was found to be valid was to be understood as right. And what was found to be invalid was not to be understood as wrong. There was no judgement, not intended and not implied. As a result nothing in this writing lays claim to even the slightest tinge of authority.

For these reasons it may be said with sincerity and with humility that incorrect Bible translations have no implications for this writing.

Thinking in words and visualisation

When we reflect on abstract topics we use words as tools because only words can hold abstract meanings. In this case we can say that we think in words.

However, physical objects or physical situations under consideration can be seen by the inner eye. They can be pictured in the mind by a person who is suitably inclined. This process may be called thinking in pictures, generally known as visualisation.

Creation or evolution?

There have been different opinions and different theories regarding the origin of the world around us and of mankind itself. On the one end of the spectrum there is the principle of creation and on the other we find the concept of evolution.

It appears to be commonly understood that creation is an event which takes place only once and that evolution is a continuous process. The world as it is and the universe as we know it appear to negate the validity of the concept of creation as a single event in the past. The changes which can be observed, the developments which have taken place over millions of years and which have been documented by scientific evidence seem to take all credibility away from the concept of creation as a single event in the past. However, the principle of evolution is not convincing either because it does not answer questions about the very beginning. Since evolution is a change of something which already exists, we are left wondering how the initial physical phenomena came into being.

Because the idea of creation by itself does not make sense and the principle of evolution on its own is found lacking, there must be something else involved. However, we seem to be mesmerised by these two theories. It is quite obvious that our thinking has been captive of its own ideas, to mean that we have once more been the prisoners of our own words, of our human language. Our thoughts have been poured into the moulds of our existing language. The abstract substance of our thoughts has been encapsulated in the physical casing of our words. Content and form have been fused to become 'meaningful' words, 'meaningful' phrases, 'meaningful' sentences.

The result of this unavoidable 'fixing' of our thoughts has been that the concept of creation is understood to exclude the concept of evolution and vice versa: both are considered to be incompatible. However, nothing could be further from the truth. The fact is that creation and evolution have been existing together and have been at work together. We can even say – we must even say – that both have been superimposed on each other, that both have been indistinguishable from each other from the very beginning.

And the very beginning was brought about by the Will of The One. Since The One is not a person who exercises a will like a human being, The One is The Will. Therefore the act of the initial creation is not just the handiwork of a god, but it is a manifestation of The One. The One manifested in two respects: The One brought about a physical existence simultaneously with a spiritual existence. The physical existence was the beginning of the universe and the spiritual existence was the Will of The One embodied in this same universe.

This simply means that the existence of the universe, at any given moment, has always been governed by the inherent Will of The One. This fact is already expressed in the opening words of the Hebrew Bible which cannot be adequately translated into English and other Indo-Germanic languages because of the special structure of the Hebrew language. These opening words of Genesis are the basis for the fundamental thoughts of Jewish theology that God established His Creation initially and that since then He has continued creating without interruption and that He will continue to create in the time to come. In other words, every day God renews the works of His Creation.(1)

Those of us who perceive only the physical aspects of the universe which is always in the making observe that 'one thing leads to another'. They very likely conclude that – at least here on earth – physical changes come about for reasons which are, directly or indirectly, attributable to physical circumstances. Particular physical changes which are considered to be gradual developments from relatively simple forms to more complex forms are then classified as evolution.

The controversy between the theories of creation and evolution consists at best of exercises of the human mind conducted without a sound basis. This is so because the ideas of creation and evolution cannot be separated when we consider the universe as it really is: a manifestation of The One.

(1) Lapide, Pinchas: op. cit., vol. 1, p 60,61

Did God create Adam?

It is always important that we are clear in our minds about the terminology we use when we think and when we express ourselves. Take the word 'create'. We can say that a potter creates beautiful vessels in his individual style. Indeed, God has been likened to a potter. And, indeed, in the Bible as we know it we read that God, taking some earth, created Adam, the first man. However, God did more than any potter can ever do, He breathed His Spirit into man.

To use the word 'create' with reference to this action of God is totally inadequate as it 'embezzles' the divine aspect. The fact is that God the Spirit presented Himself to the world in the physical forms of Adam and Eve. This actually means that God made Himself perceptible, even tangible: God manifested in human form.

In the Bible as we know it this event is presented in the First Book of Moses 1: 27 where we read: 'So God created man in his own image, in the image of God he created him; male and female he created them.' At first glance quite a puzzling statement and forever after potentially quite misleading. Do we appear to be like God? Even more so, does God appear to be like us? As a matter of fact, the just God does and so does the angry one, the punishing one, the rewarding one, the fear-inspiring one, the loving one to his followers, the condemning one to the unbelievers, the forgiving one and the unforgiving one – the God of our fathers and, one might add, the God of our mothers: the human God.

How wonderfully different is the God who has revealed Himself since the days the Bible was written. How wonderfully different is the God who does no create like a human being, but manifests only: always manifests as The One.

Is the Good News for modern man in today's Bible?

Occasionally I had come across opinions and theories which cast doubt on the way we think of Jesus as a historical figure. The ordinary layman, I think, cannot avoid forming a certain picture of the man Jesus through reading and hearing what is written about Him in the Bible as we know it. I have never felt that historical theories and uncertainties about Jesus had any bearing on the certainty of my faith.

Until about six years ago I was not at all sensitive to the contradictions which are found in the Bible as we know it. It was not until I began reading the German Luther Bible and a little later also the French Bible simultaneously with the Authorised Version that I realised that there can also be contradictions between Bibles of different languages. These contradictions are obviously due to differences of translation and interpretation. Now there was an added uncertainty: the doubt about the word. And that definitely had a bearing on my faith. Although I have never believed according to the letter of the word, when the words become doubtful, the meanings behind these words begin to stir.(1)

I gratefully count my blessings that I was taken by the hand, so to speak, and led through unknown territory out into the open spaces where everything looks exactly as it really is. No ambiguity, no blurred outlines, no thoughts going round in circles, no juggling of words, nothing but refreshing clarity. I was granted the privilege to be given – what I would like to call – a correspondence course in matters spiritual.

As I was writing I was being taught. For a while the words of the Bible as we know it provided topics and thoughts about which I was given information. This information was sometimes just a temporary measure, a kind of stop-gap knowledge which was again dismantled later on when it had done its job. Now I realise that I was gradually being weaned from the words and introduced more and more to the thoughts which had been buried under layers of these used, abused, tormented and worn-out words.

When I recorded the chapter 'The nature of our spiritual awareness' in 1994, it was like writing about something which lay far off in the future. Now I have caught up with it, four and a half years later. When I recorded the chapter 'Is faith without works dead?' in 1997, I was thrilled with it. However, I realise only now that it provided the spiritual rock on which I firmly stand. Now I recognise and acknowledge it as my credo.

Pinchas Lapide's writings must cause many people confusion and heartache, a deep sense of loss and a great spiritual uncertainty. May these people be granted the courage, the strength and the help so that they can open their hearts to the changes which have been taking shape for quite a while and for which it was time to see the light of day. Pinchas Lapide has done me personally a great favour. In a scholarly and convincing way he has shown that for reasons of authenticity alone it is impossible to tie one's faith to the wording of the Bible as we know it and to be closely connected with The One at the same time.

Because in the Bible as we know it there is no emphasis on the divine nature of man's soul, because the existence of The One is not acknowledged, there is also no possibility for Divine Unconditional Love. As a result, there cannot be the progressive development of faith which is sustained by the increasing awareness of the Presence of The One. Indeed, it is this kind of faith, this kind of bonding between man and The One which is the *true* 'Good News for Modern Man' – but the believer does not find it in today's Bible.(2)

(1)   It was the passage of John 3: 16-18 which really made me take notice. In verse 18 we read: 'He who believes in him *is not condemned*; he who does not believe *is condemned already,* because he has not believed in the name of the only Son of God.'

The German Bible and the French Bible use different expressions to render the statements italicised above. In both 'is not condemned' is given as 'is not judged' and 'is condemned already' is given as 'is judged already'.

(2)   The New Testament in today's English published by the American Bible Society (1966) is called 'Good News for Modern Man'.

It may be of interest here to mention that the Old English form of our word 'gospel' was 'godspel'. Originally the vowel 'o' was long because the first part of 'godspel' meant 'good': 'godspel' = 'good news, good tidings'. Later on this vowel 'o' became short making the first part sound like 'god, God'.

Postscript

In their minds some readers may like to replace the term 'Unconditional

161

Love' with the expression 'Divine Compassion' because they feel more comfortable with it.

Conclusion

This writing has concerned itself directly and indirectly with the relationship between man's soul and The One.

When we have progressed sufficiently along the path of our spiritual journey the pulsating flow of spiritual energy between The One and our soul excludes quite emphatically anything which is of physical nature, of worldly substance. There is absolutely no need anywhere for a mediator, nor is there any room for one. There is only The One, man's soul and the Unconditional Love of The One.

What is man
that thou art mindful
of him?

This question from Psalm 8 was one of the first discoveries among the Bible quotations used in this writing. It immediately offered itself as the title, but later took on the role of one of the fundamental themes running through this book. And the whole book responds to this age-old question with the momentous answer:

Man is
the manifestation of The One
in human form.

In conclusion may I express the wish and the hope that the reader will find that this book will help him to become more and more aware of the wonderful gift which is there for each and every one of us: our unassailable bond with The One.

The LORD bless you and keep you:
The LORD make his face to shine
upon you, and be gracious to you:
The LORD lift up his countenance
upon you, and give you peace.
(4 Moses 6: 24-26)

BIBLIOGRAPHY

The following books were used in connection with this writing:

The Holy Bible, Revised Standard Version, Revised 1952
  (The British and Foreign Bible Society)
Die Bibel, Nach der Übersetzung Martin Luthers
  (The Bible, According to Martin Luther's Translation)
  In der revidierten Fassung von 1984
  (Revised edition of 1984)
  Deutsche Bibelgesellschaft, Stuttgart
  (German Bible Society, Stuttgart)
La Bible, Traduction œcuménique de la Bible
  (The Bible, Ecumenical Translation of the Bible)
  Nouvelle édition revue 1992
  (New edition revised 1992)
  Alliance Biblique Universelle – Le Cerf
  (Universal Bible Alliance – Le Cerf)
*Good News for Modern Man, The New Testament in Today's
  English Version*
  (The American Bible Society 1966)
Neukirchener Kalender
  (A calendar published by the Education Society of
  Neukirchen-Vluyn, Germany, for the Lutheran and
  Reformed Evangelical Churches of Germany and
  Switzerland)
Chambers Etymological English Dictionary
  Edited by A. M. MacDonald
  (W. & R. Chambers, Ltd., 1967; Edinburgh)
Fuller, Simon Peter: *Rising Out of Chaos . . . The New Heaven and the
  New Earth*
  (Kima Global, Ltd., Rondebosch, South Africa 1994)

Lapide, Pinchas: *Ist die Bibel richtig übersetzt?* Band 1, Band 2,
    (*Has the Bible Been Translated Correctly?* Vols 1 and 2)
    Gütersloher Verlagshaus, Gütersloh, 1986 und 1994
    (Gütersloh Publishing House, Gütersloh, Germany; 1986
    and 1994)
Robinson, Thomas: *The Bible Timeline,*
    (Michael Friedman Publishing Group Inc., New York; 1992)
The Columbia Encyclopedia
    Edited by W. Bridgwater and E. J. Sherwood
    (Columbia University Press, New York; Second Edition, 1950)
The Universal Dictionary of the English Language
    Edited by Henry Cecil Wyld
    (Routlege & Kegan Paul Limited; London; Fourteenth
    Impression, 1961)